LET MY PEOPLE GO SURFING

LET MY PEOPLE GO SURFING

The Education of a Reluctant Businessman

Yvon Chouinard

Founder and Owner, Patagonia, Inc.

THE PENGUIN PRESS | NEW YORK | 2005

THE PENGUIN PRESS
Published by the Penguin Group
Penguin Group (USA) Inc., 375 Hudson Street, New York, New York 10014, U.S.A. •
Penguin Group (Canada), 90 Eglinton Avenue East, Suite 700, Toronto, Ontario, Canada M4P 2Y3
(a division of Pearson Penguin Canada Inc.) • Penguin Books Ltd, 80 Strand,
London WC2R 0RL, England • Penguin Ireland, 25 St. Stephen's Green, Dublin 2,
Ireland (a division of Penguin Books Ltd) • Penguin Books Australia Ltd, 250 Camberwell Road,
Camberwell, Victoria 3124, Australia (a division of Pearson Australia Group Pty Ltd) •
Penguin Books India Pvt Ltd, 11 Community Centre, Panchsheel Park, New Delhi –
110 017, India • Penguin Group (NZ), Cnr Airborne and Rosedale Roads, Albany,
Auckland 1310, New Zealand (a division of Pearson New Zealand Ltd) •
Penguin Books (South Africa) (Pty) Ltd, 24 Sturdee Avenue,
Rosebank, Johannesburg 2196, South Africa

Penguin Books Ltd, Registered Offices:
80 Strand, London WC2R 0RL, England

First published in 2005 by The Penguin Press, a member of Penguin Group (USA) Inc.

5   7   9   10   8   6

Page 263 constitutes an extension of this copyright page.

The pages of this book are printed on paper that is both FSC
certified and recycled (containing 35 percent postconsumer waste).
The FSC Logo identifies forests which have been certified in
accordance with the rules of the Forest Stewardship Council.

Mixed Sources
Product group from well-managed
forests and other controlled sources
www.fsc.org Cert no. SCS-COC-00648
© 1996 Forest Stewardship Council

LIBRARY OF CONGRESS CATALOGING IN PUBLICATION DATA

Chouinard, Yvon.
Let my people go surfing : the education of a reluctant businessman / Yvon Chouinard.
p.   cm.
ISBN 1-59420-072-6
1. Chouinard, Yvon.   2. Businesspeople—United States—Biography.
3. Social responsibility of business.   I. Title.
HC102.5.C42 2005
658.4'083–dc22   2005047650

Printed in the United States of America
DESIGNED BY AMANDA DEWEY

For Malinda Pennoyer Chouinard,

my wife and partner

for all these good years

CONTENTS

INTRODUCTION   1

HISTORY   5

PHILOSOPHIES   81

   PRODUCT DESIGN PHILOSOPHY   85

   PRODUCTION PHILOSOPHY   117

   DISTRIBUTION PHILOSOPHY   126

   IMAGE PHILOSOPHY   147

   FINANCIAL PHILOSOPHY   159

   HUMAN RESOURCE PHILOSOPHY   165

   MANAGEMENT PHILOSOPHY   177

   ENVIRONMENTAL PHILOSOPHY   187

1% FOR THE PLANET ALLIANCE   247

SUMMARY   253

THANK YOU . . .   261

INTRODUCTION

've been a businessman for almost fifty years. It's as difficult for me to say those words as it is for someone to admit being an alcoholic or a lawyer. I've never respected the profession. It's business that has to take the majority of the blame for being the enemy of nature, for destroying native cultures, for taking from the poor and giving to the rich, and for poisoning the earth with the effluent from its factories.

Yet business can produce food, cure disease, control population, employ people, and generally enrich our lives. And it can do these good things and make a profit without losing its soul. That's what this book is about.

Like many people who had their formative years in the sixties in America, I grew up with disdain for big corporations and their lackey governments. The typical young Republican's dream of making more money than his parents or of starting a business, growing it as fast as possible, taking it public, and retiring to the golf courses of Leisure World has never appealed to me. My values are a result of living a life close to nature and being passionately involved in doing what some people would call risky sports.

My wife, Malinda, and I and the other contrarian employees of Patagonia have taken lessons learned from these sports and our alternative lifestyle and applied them to running a company.

My company, Patagonia, Inc., is an experiment. It exists to put into action those recommendations that all the doomsday books on the health of our home planet say we must do immediately to avoid the certain destruction of nature and collapse of our civilization. Despite near-universal consensus among scientists that we are on the brink of an environmental collapse, our society lacks the will to take action. We're collectively paralyzed by apathy, inertia, or lack of imagination. Patagonia exists to challenge conventional wisdom and present a new style of responsible business. We believe the accepted model of capitalism that necessitates endless growth and deserves the blame for the destruction of nature must be displaced. Patagonia and its thousand employees have the means and the will to prove to the rest of the business world that doing the right thing makes for good and profitable business.

This book has been in process for fifteen years because it's taken that long to prove to ourselves that we can break the rules of traditional business and make it not just work but work even better, especially for a company that wants to be here for the next one hundred years.

HISTORY
HISTORY

No young kid growing up ever dreams of someday becoming a businessman. He wants to be a fireman, a sponsored athlete, or a forest ranger. The Lee Iacoccas, Donald Trumps, and Jack Welches of the business world are heroes to no one except other businessmen with similar values. I wanted to be a fur trapper when I grew up.

My father was a tough French Canadian from Quebec. Papa completed only three years of schooling before he had to begin working on the family farm, at the age of nine. In later years he worked as a journeyman plasterer, carpenter, electrician, and plumber. In Lisbon, Maine, where I was born, he repaired all the looms at the Worumbo Woolen Mill. One of the profound memories of my early childhood was seeing him sitting in the kitchen next to the wood-burning stove, drinking a bottle of whiskey, and proceeding to pull out some of his teeth, both good and bad, with his electrician's pliers. He needed dentures but thought the local dentist was asking too much money for the part of the job he could just as easily do himself.

I think I must have learned to climb before I could walk; Father Simard, who lived upstairs in a house we were renting, encouraged me to crawl up the stairs, where I was rewarded with a spoonful of honey. When I was about six, my brother, Gerald, took me out fishing and sneaked a ten-inch pickerel onto the end of the line and made believe I caught it. I've been hooked on fishing ever since.

Nearly everyone was French Canadian in Lisbon, and I attended a French-speaking Catholic school until I was seven.

My two sisters, Doris and Rachel, were nine and eleven years older, and since my brother was in the military and my father was always working, I was brought up surrounded by women. I have ever since preferred that accommodation. My mother, Yvonne, was the adventurous one in the family, and it was her idea to move the family in 1946 to California, where she hoped the dry climate would be better for my father's asthma.

We auctioned off all our possessions, including the hand-built furniture my father had made, and one traumatic day the six of us piled into the family Chrysler and drove west. Somewhere along Route 66 we stopped at an Indian hogan, and my mother took out the preserved corn she had put up for the trip and gave it all to a Hopi woman and her hungry children. That incident was probably my first lesson in philanthropy.

When we arrived in Burbank, we stayed with another French Canadian family and I was put in a public school. I was the smallest kid in the class, I couldn't speak English, and I constantly had to defend myself because I had a "girl's" name. So I did what any future entrepreneur probably would have done: I ran away.

My parents transferred me to a parochial school, where I was able to get more help from the nuns. My report card from that year showed Ds in every subject. The language and cultural differences made me a loner, and I spent most of my time off by myself. Before the other kids in my neighborhood were even allowed

La famille Chouinard on our first day in California. 1946. *Courtesy of Patagonia*

to cross the street on their own, I was bicycling seven or eight miles to reach a lake on a private golf course, where I hid in the willows away from the guards and fished for bluegills and bass. Later on I discovered the urban wilds of Griffith Park and the Los Angeles River, where I spent every day after school gigging frogs, trapping crawdads, and hunting cottontails with my bow and arrow. In the summer we swam in a foam-filled swimming hole fed by an outflow pipe from the film developing labs at one of the movie studios. If I ever get cancer, it can probably be traced back to that time.

High school was the worst. I had pimples, I couldn't dance, and I had no interest in any of the subjects except for the shop classes. I had an "attitude" and was always in detention. I excelled at athletics like baseball and football, but when it came time to perform while people were watching, I would fumble the ball. I

Some of the members of the Southern California Falconry Club.
That's me with a goshawk on the right. 1956. *Courtesy of Patagonia*

learned at an early age that it's better to invent your own game; then you can always be a winner. I found my games in the ocean, creeks, and hillsides surrounding Los Angeles.

Math was so boring at times I'd just stare at the ceiling and try to count all the holes in the perforated soundboard. History class was an opportunity for me to practice holding my breath, so that on weekends I could free-dive deeper to catch the abundant abalone and lobster off the Malibu coast. In auto shop class I would lie on the creeper, slide under the car I was working on, and come out only to check out the legs on the cute girl who came to take the roll.

Some fellow misfits, along with adults like Robert Klimes, a music teacher, and Tom Cade, a graduate student at UCLA, started the Southern California Falconry Club, where we trained hawks and falcons for hunting. Every weekend in the spring we went off looking for hawk nests; sometimes we banded the young for the government or we took a young hawk to train. Our club was responsible for enacting the first falconry regulations in California.

It was the most formative time of my life. When a fifteen-year-old has to trap a wild goshawk, stay up all night with her until the bird finally develops enough trust to fall asleep on his fist, and then train the proud bird using only positive reinforcement, well, the Zen master would have to ask, "Just who is getting trained here?"

One of the adults, Don Prentice, was a climber, and he taught us how to rappel down to the falcon aeries on the cliffs. We had always just held on to the rope and climbed down hand over hand, but he showed us how to wrap manila rope (stolen from the telephone company) around the hip and over the shoulder to control the slide down. We thought it was the greatest sport ever, and we kept practicing, improving, and

Practice rappelling at Stony Point, San Fernando Valley. Early fifties. *Courtesy of Patagonia*

innovating. We made our own leather-padded rappelling clothes so we could go faster and faster.

We hopped freight trains to the west end of the San Fernando Valley in order to practice rappelling on the sandstone cliffs of Stony Point. We had no specialized gear or climbing boots. We just wore sneakers or went barefoot.

We had never thought about trying to climb up the cliffs until one day when I was rappelling down a chimney on Stony Point and came across this fellow from the Sierra Club climbing up! We got Don Prentice to show us a few more pointers about climbing, and that June—I was sixteen then—I drove to Wyoming in my 1940 Ford, which I had rebuilt in auto shop class. I remember the great feeling I had driving alone through the Nevada desert, in hundred-degree temperatures, passing by the Oldsmobiles and Cadillacs stopped by the side of the road with their hoods up, overheating.

I met up with Don Prentice and some other young fellows in Pinedale, Wyoming, and we backpacked into the northern Wind River Range. We wanted to climb Gannett Peak, the highest mountain in Wyoming, but there were no guidebooks, and we kind of got lost. I wanted to go up the west side, and the others wanted to go up some gullies to the north. We split up, and I soloed up some cliff bands on the West Face. Late in the day I ended up alone at the summit, in a thunderstorm, slipping around the snowfields in my smooth-soled Sears work boots.

From there I drove up to the Tetons to spend the rest of the summer learning to climb. I eventually talked my way into joining two guys from Dartmouth who were planning a climb up Templeton's Crack on Symmetry Spire. This was after other climbers had turned me down for my lack of experience, so I didn't elaborate on my history. This would be my first actual roped climb, but I just faked it and pushed ahead, even when they asked me to lead the most difficult pitch, a wet, slimy crack. They handed me pitons and a hammer I had no idea how to use,

Glenn Exum. Mountain guide, music teacher, and superb dry fly trout fisherman. 1983.
Courtesy of Patagonia

but I figured it out and managed anyway. After that trip I returned to the Tetons every summer to climb for three months. Looking back now on those early attempts at climbing, I sometimes think it's a miracle I survived.

I also fished in the Tetons. When I was seventeen, I saw Glenn Exum teaching his son, Eddie, how to fly cast over by the climbing school shack. Glenn was a mountain guide and a climbing legend in the valley. He was also an elegant caster and a superb dry fly fisherman. When he saw me watching, he yelled, "Come on over here, son!" and proceeded to teach me to cast with a fly. I put away my spinning rod and superduper lures and have fished exclusively with flies ever since.

We lived in this beach shack in San Blas, Mexico, for a month in 1957, eating fish and tropical fruit, swatting no-see-ums, mosquitoes, and scorpions, waxing our surfboards with votive candles from the local church.
Courtesy of Patagonia

Back in California, I started hanging out at Stony Point on weekends in the winter and at Tahquitz Rock above Palm Springs in the fall and spring. There I met some young climbers of the Sierra Club: TM Herbert, Royal Robbins, Tom Frost, Bob Kamps, and others. Eventually, we migrated from Tahquitz to Yosemite, where few of the big walls had been climbed.

After graduating from high school in 1956, I attended a community college for two years and worked part-time for my brother, who ran a private detective business, Mike Conrad and Associates. The main client was Howard Hughes, and it was mostly hanky-panky–type stuff: keeping track of Hughes's innumerable young "starlets," guarding a yacht to keep it "germ-free," and keeping him well hidden so he couldn't be subpoenaed for a lawsuit over Trans World Airlines.

During school holidays I would go with friends down to the wilds of Baja and the coastal mainland of Mexico to surf, driving the '39 Chevy I'd bought for fifteen dollars. After getting nineteen flats on one trip, we stuffed our back tires with brush and weeds and inched the last dozen miles into Mazatlán. We were always sick from the bad water and couldn't afford medicine, so we would powder charcoal from the campfire, mix it with a cup of salt in a glass of water, and drink that as an emetic.

I soon realized that if I was going to spend the rest of my life drinking bad water and eating out of the street vendors and bazaars of the third world, I'd better get used to it. Developing a natural immunity to the *turistas* and giardia is not an easy passage, but if you refuse to take Flagyl and antibiotics and don't drink iodine-treated or chlorinated water, the immunity gradually happens. It's sort of homeopathic. Even today I drink out of every stream I fish in, and I rarely get sick.

In 1957 I went to a junkyard and bought a used coal-fired forge, a 138-pound anvil, and some tongs and hammers and started teaching myself blacksmithing. I wanted to make my own climbing hardware, since we were starting to climb the big walls in Yosemite on multiday ascents that required hundreds of piton placements. The soft iron pitons imported from Europe were meant to be placed once

Pioneer Yosemite climber and blacksmith John Salethé. The brand for his Peninsula Ironworks was a traditional "Diamond P," which was the inspiration for the Chouinard Equipment "Diamond C." *Courtesy of Patagonia*

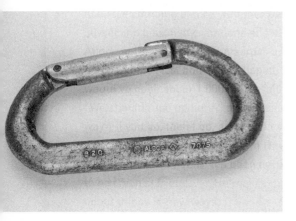

The first Chouinard carabiners were entirely machined on a Sears & Roebuck drill press. *Courtesy of Patagonia*

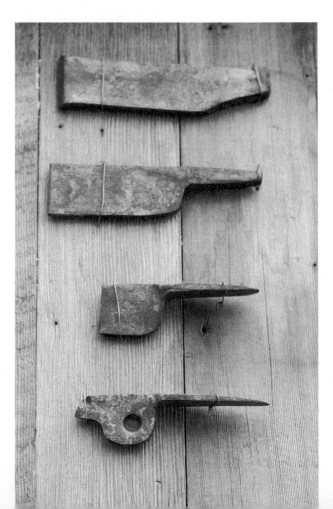

The progression of forging a piton from 4130 chrome-molybdenum steel bar stocks. *Courtesy of Patagonia*

and left in the rock. Better pitons had once been made out of old Model A Ford axles by John Salathé, a Swiss blacksmith and climber who had used them on the first ascent of Lost Arrow Chimney in Yosemite, but he had stopped making them.

I made my first pitons from an old chrome-molybdenum steel blade from a harvester, and TM Herbert and I used them on early ascents of the Lost Arrow Chimney and the North Face of Sentinel Rock in Yosemite. These stiffer and stronger pitons were ideal for driving into the often incipient cracks in Yosemite and could be taken out and used over and over again. I

Forging pitons outside my first shop in Burbank. The surfboard in the background I made from balsa wood and fiberglass. I eventually traded it for a Model A Ford engine. 1957. *Dan Doody*

made these Lost Arrow pitons for myself and the few friends I climbed with; then friends of friends wanted some. I could forge two of my chrome-molybdenum steel pitons in an hour, and I started selling them for $1.50 each. You could buy European pitons for 20 cents, but you had to have my new gear if you wanted to do the state-of-the-art climbs that we were doing.

I also wanted to make a stronger carabiner, so in 1957 I borrowed $825.35 from my parents to pay for a drop forging die. I drove to the Aluminum Company of America headquarters in Los Angeles. I was eighteen years old, had a full beard, Levi's huarache sandals, and a fistful of cash right down to the thirty-five cents. The people at ALCOA hardly knew how to process cash through their system, but they made my drop forging die.

My father helped me build a small shop out of an old chicken coop in our backyard in Burbank. Most of my tools were portable, so I would load up my car and travel up and down the California coast from Big Sur to San Diego. I would surf, then haul my anvil down to the beach and cut out angle pitons with a cold chisel and hammer before moving on to another surfing beach. I found gas money by diving into trash cans and redeeming soda pop bottles.

For the next few years I worked on my equipment in the winter months, spent April to July on the walls of Yosemite, headed out of the heat of summer for the high mountains of Wyoming, Canada, and the Alps and then back to Yosemite in the fall until the snow fell in November. During these times I supported myself selling the equipment from the back of my car. The profits were slim, though. For weeks at a time I'd live on fifty cents to a dollar a day. Before leaving for the Rockies one summer, my friend Ken Weeks and I bought a couple of cases of dented cat food cans from a damaged can outlet in San Francisco. We supplemented the cat food with oatmeal, potatoes, ground squirrel, blue grouse, and porcupines assassinated à la Trotsky with an ice ax. I slept two hundred days a year or more in my old army-surplus sleeping bag. I didn't buy a tent until I was almost forty, preferring to sleep under boulders and under the low-hanging branches of an alpine fir.

In Yosemite we called ourselves the Valley Cong. We hid out from the rangers in nooks and crannies behind Camp 4 when we overstayed the two-week camping limit. We took special pride in the fact that climbing rocks and icefalls had no economic value in society. We were rebels from the consumer culture. Politicians and businessmen were "greaseballs," and corporations were the source of all evil. The natural world was our home. Our heroes were Muir, Thoreau, and Emerson and the European climbers Gaston Rebuffat, Ricardo Cassin, and Herman Buhl. We were like the wild species living on the edge of an ecosystem—adaptable, resilient, and tough.

In the fall of 1962, coming back from climbing on the East Coast, Chuck Pratt and I were arrested for riding a freight train in Winslow, Arizona, and we spent

My climbing partner Ken Weeks and I cleaned out this incinerator and lived in it one summer in the Tetons of Wyoming. 1958.
Lorraine Bonney

Camping in the Tetons. That's not my sissy air mattress. 1958.
Courtesy of Patagonia

With my Korean climbing friends in front
of In So Bong peak near Seoul. 1963.
Courtesy of Patagonia

eighteen days in jail. The charge was "wandering around aimlessly with no apparent means of support." By the time we got out, we had each lost twenty pounds on the jailhouse diet of Wonder bread, beans, and oatmeal. We had only fifteen cents between us, it was snowing, and the cops gave us a half hour to get out of town. Yet we never entertained the thought of calling our parents or friends for help. Climbing had taught us to be self-reliant; there were no rescue teams in those days.

A few weeks later I was called up for the draft. I tried to fail the physical by drinking a big bottle of soy sauce in order to raise my blood pressure, but I got so sick I couldn't keep it down. I was inducted and sent to Fort Ord. Disliking authority and angry about having to close down my little climbing business, I didn't get along well with the army. Its logic, since my occupation was "blacksmith," was to try to make me into a Nike missile system mechanic. After basic training, I hastily married a local Burbank girl before being shipped off to Korea, where I caused nothing but trouble by "forgetting" to salute officers, looking slovenly, going on hunger strikes, and generally acting unbalanced but always backing off just shy of risking court-martial. The army finally sent me off to work with some civilians where all I had to do was turn their generator on and off every day. I had plenty of free time, so I would sneak off with several young Korean climbers to put up first ascents all over the smooth granite domes and pinnacles north of Seoul.

Miraculously, I was honorably discharged in 1964. I came home to a failed marriage and went straight to the Yosemite Valley to make the ten-day first ascent of the North American Wall on El Capitan with Chuck Pratt, Tom Frost, and Royal Robbins. At the time, it was probably the hardest big wall climb in the world. In the fall of that year I started making my climbing gear again and moved the operation into a tin shed near the Lockheed aircraft plant in Burbank. That year I put out my first catalog, a one-page mimeographed list of items and prices, with a blunt disclaimer on the bottom saying not to expect fast delivery during the months of May to November.

The overhanging North American Wall of El Capitan, named after the dark area of rock that resembles a map of the Americas. *Tom Frost*

Traversing to the Black Diahedral
(the seventeenth pitch). 1964. *Tom Frost*

Tom Frost on top, Royal Robbins and me peeking
out of the bottom, bivouacking under the Great
Roof. My parents knew I was a climber but didn't
know what that meant until one day on the
evening TV news they watched a helicopter scan
the face of El Capitan and zero in on these crazy
guys sleeping in hammocks two thousand feet off
the ground. *Chuck Pratt*

I hired my first "employees," climbing friends like Layton Kor, Gary Hemming, Bill Johnson, Tony Jesson, and Dennis Hennek. Most of the work consisted of forging, grinding, and crude machining. In 1966 I moved from Burbank to Ventura to be close to the point surf breaks of Ventura and Santa Barbara. I set up shop in a rented tin boiler room of an abandoned packing company slaughterhouse.

Demand for my gear grew until I couldn't keep up making it by hand, so I started using more sophisticated tools and dies and machinery. I went into partnership with Tom and Doreen Frost. Tom was an aeronautical engineer who had a keen sense of design and aesthetics. Doreen handled the bookkeeping and business end of things. During the nine years that the Frosts and I were partners, we redesigned and improved just about every climbing tool, making each one stronger, lighter, simpler, and

FROM THE SEVENTEENTH PITCH OF THE NORTH AMERICAN WALL, OCTOBER 1964

Getting dark fast . . . as usual we will have to climb in the dark. It really gets on your nerves, can't even see to make a correct knot.

Pratt Prussics up to me and hangs a few feet below, waiting to haul as Frost leads up under an overhang to a dirty rotten flaky corner. Everybody's really nervous. Tom does a fantastic job of nailing this dangerous pitch in record time. He makes it to the Great Roof and places a bolt and several pitons.

I clear the pitch, in absolute darkness, by feel and by light of the occasional spark from the hammer hitting the pitons. Have to leave in two pins. My fingers are swollen like little fat sausages and my wrists ache from the nailing, but more than anything I'm frightened by this having to climb in the dark.

I put in another anchor. What an incredible place we are in—a huge dihedral that ends under a twenty-five-foot ceiling. The wall below overhangs the base of the cliff so much that there's no possibility of retreat from here, much less from above this roof *if* we can even get over it. By midnight we have set up our hammocks one above another. Robbins's and Pratt's hammocks bridge the two walls of the corner. Good bivouac, though, and we all sleep well from sheer exhaustion.

—Y.C.

My second shop in Burbank was just some open metal sheds,
but I was beginning to get into assembly-line production.
1965. *Courtesy of Patagonia*

more functional. Quality control was always foremost in our minds, because if a
tool failed, it could kill someone, and since we were our own best customers, there
was a good chance it would be *us*! Our guiding principle of design stemmed from
Antoine de Saint Exupéry, the French aviator:

> Have you ever thought, not only about the airplane but whatever
> man builds, that all of man's industrial efforts, all his computations
> and calculations, all the nights spent working over draughts and blue-

prints, invariably culminate in the production of a thing whose sole and guiding principle is the ultimate principle of simplicity?

It is as if there were a natural law which ordained that to achieve this end, to refine the curve of a piece of furniture, or a ship's keel, or the fuselage of an airplane, until gradually it partakes of the elementary purity of the curve of the human breast or shoulder, there must be experimentation of several generations of craftsmen. In anything at all, perfection is finally attained not when there is no longer anything to add, but when there is no longer anything to take away, when a body has been stripped down to its nakedness.

At the base of a mountain wall, where you spread out your gear to organize for a climb, it was easy to spot the tools made by Chouinard Equipment. Ours stood out because they had the cleanest lines. They were also the lightest, strongest, and most versatile tools in use. Where other designers would work to improve a tool's performance by adding on, Tom Frost and I would achieve the same ends by taking away—reducing weight and bulk without sacrificing strength or the level of protection.

We continued to hire friends, as we needed more help. In the mid-1960s Roger McDivitt and his sister, Kris, lived a couple of doors away on the surfing beach, where I was renting a little cabin for seventy-five dollars a month. Kris began working for us first, as an assistant packer, and Roger, when he returned from Vietnam as a young officer with three Purple Hearts, started working in the blacksmith shop.

With a degree in economics, Roger had a natural aptitude for business and rapidly moved from doing shop work to wholesale and retail sales and eventually became general manager. His first job was peening over the rivets on bong bongs. These are big-angle pitons for wide cracks, and the rivet heads had to be peened, or pounded smooth, with a hammer. Roger would find a nice place out in the

The Ventura shop employees in 1966. Tom, Doreen, Tony, Dennis, Terry, Yvon, Merl, and Davey. *Tom Frost*

sunny courtyard that wasn't occupied by a dog or one of the other employees, then sit on the ground and hammer on these rivets all day long, taking great care to make a nice round peen.

Climbers used to drop in to buy our gear from us, and eventually Roger handled these retail sales. That duty grew into wholesale sales as well. Our first retail store was another ugly tin shed, and it was Roger's idea to swipe some old wooden fencing from a nearby ranch, combine it with some wood from the crates that our imported ropes came in, and decorate the inside of the store with the old wood. Roger became our first general manager, for four years, and then his sister, Kris, took over when he went on to manage our production.

Roger showed his business acumen at an early age. One day in the early seventies, he took ten boxes of brand-new pitons behind the shop. They were a combination of Lost Arrows, Bugaboos, and Angles, all chrome-moly steel models. Roger took a large handful of pitons from one of the boxes, connected them all to a rope, and proceeded to drag them around and around on the concrete. I asked him what in the world he was doing.

He explained that this was an export shipment to Graham Tiso in Edinburgh, Scotland, our distributor for the UK at the time. Roger explained that after roughing up the pitons, he would soak them in a barrel of vinegar and water for a few days, then remove them to dry and rust in the open air. They could then be exported to the UK as scrap metal, without being subject to customs duties. Upon receipt of the pitons, Tiso would polish and oil them until they were like new and sell them at a price that was affordable even for dirtbag British climbers.

My favorite memory of Roger is from a time when we were living hand to mouth and the usual deadbeat dealers were not paying their bills. One day one of our more important dealers sent in a new order, even though

From this funky shop we produced the finest climbing tools in the world. C. 1970. *Tom Frost*

Ellen Malinda Pennoyer camping in Yosemite. C. 1969.
Courtesy of Patagonia

his outstanding balance was way overdue. Roger went out back to the machine shop and gathered up bits of miscellaneous junk steel and lead pipes from around the blacksmith shop floor, then disappeared into the shipping room. He packed all the scrap metal in a large box and shipped it COD for the amount of the outstanding balance. A few days later, when the irate dealer called in to complain, Roger calmly told him we were now even and he was once again a dealer in good standing— although only for COD orders.

In 1968 Tom and Doreen covered for me while I took a six-month road trip from Ventura to the tip of South America, surfing the west coast of the Americas down to Lima, skiing volcanoes in Chile, and climbing Mount Fitzroy in Patagonia, Argentina. The next year Tom went off to the Himalayas for several months to climb the South Face of Annapurna, in Nepal. Doreen and I watched over the business while he was away.

Since there wasn't much profit at the end of the year, we paid ourselves by the hours worked. None of us saw the business as an end in itself. It was just a way to pay the bills so we could go off on climbing trips.

During this time I met Malinda Pennoyer, an art student at Fresno State College and a weekend cabin maid at Yosemite Lodge. She rock climbed just enough to attract the attention of an itinerant blacksmith/climber. When we married in 1970, Malinda was teaching art in high school, but she soon became involved in the business. From May to October, when the owners took over the beach shack we rented, Malinda and I lived in the back of an old van in the courtyard when we weren't traveling, until she fashioned an apartment for us in the basement under our retail store. She comanaged that store for a while with our infant son, Fletcher, strapped to her back.

All the while we were doubling our sales each year, and eventually we couldn't

Tom Frost and me at the forge. Ventura. C. 1970. *Courtesy of Patagonia*

Sorting out the gear for a big wall attempt in the "iron" age. 1964.
Courtesy of Patagonia

keep up by hiring our itinerant climbing friends, who were content to work only until they had enough money to go off themselves and climb. So we hired some more reliable Korean climbers whom I had climbed with in the army, some Mexican workers, and an Argentine machinist, Julio Varela, who was hiding out from the INS.

Despite the volume of sales, Chouinard Equipment for alpinists showed only about a 1 percent profit at the end of the year. Because we were constantly coming up with new designs, we would scrap after one year tools and dies that should have been amortized over three or five years. At least we didn't have much competition; no one else was foolish enough to want to get into that market. By 1970

Chouinard Equipment had become the largest supplier of climbing hardware in the United States.

It had also started down the path to becoming an environmental villain. The popularity of climbing, though growing steadily, remained concentrated on the same well-tried routes in leading areas such as El Dorado Canyon near Boulder, the Shawangunks in New York, and Yosemite Valley. The repeated hammering of hard steel pitons, during both placement and removal in the same fragile cracks, was severely disfiguring the rock. After an ascent of the Nose route on El Capitan, which had been pristine a few summers earlier, I came home disgusted with the degradation I had seen. Frost and I decided we would phase out the piton business. This was to be the first big environmental step we were to take over the years. Pitons were the mainstay of our business, but we were destroying the very rocks we loved.

Fortunately, there was an alternative to pitons: aluminum chocks that could be wedged by hand rather than hammered in and out of cracks. British climbers had been using them on their crags, but because they were crude, they were little known and less trusted in the rest of Europe and the States. We designed our own versions, called Stoppers and Hexentrics, and sold them in small quantities until the appearance of the first Chouinard Equipment catalog in 1972.

The catalog opened with "A word . . . ," an editorial from the owners on the environmental hazards of pitons. A fourteen-page essay on clean climbing by Sierra climber Doug Robinson on how to use chocks began with a powerful paragraph: "There is a word for it, and the word is clean. Climbing with only nuts and runners for protection is clean climbing. Clean because the rock is left unaltered by the passing climber. Clean because nothing is hammered into the rock and then hammered back out, leaving the rock scarred and the next climber's experience less natural. Clean because the climber's protection leaves little trace of his ascension. Clean is climbing the rock without changing it; a step closer to organic climbing for the natural man."

Malinda, Yvon, and son, Fletcher, in Yosemite. C. 1975.
The Nose route of El Capitan is elegantly profiled
in the left background. *Courtesy of Patagonia*

We faced resistance from older climbers, who were used to pounding in pitons to the hilt with their twenty-ounce hammers, and protests from young climbers, who said that we had used pitons for all our big wall climbs and now were asking them to use only these little pieces of machined aluminum "nuts." To prove our point, a young climber, Bruce Carson, and I went back up the Nose route on El Capitan without any hammers or pitons and placed only chocks and used the few bolts and pitons that were "fixed."

Within a few months of the cata-log's mailing, the piton business had atrophied; chocks sold faster than they could be made. In the tin buildings of Chouinard Equipment, the steady pounding rhythm of the drop hammer gave way to the high-pitched, searing whine of the multiple drill jig.

Then came my first idea for cloth-ing. In the late sixties, after crag climb-ing in the Peak District in England, I stopped by an old Lancashire mill that contained the last machine left in the world that still made a tough, super-heavy corduroy cloth. The mill dated back to the Industrial Revolution, when it had been water-powered. Back then, before denim, workmen's pants used to be made of corduroy because its tufted wales protected the woven backing from abrasion and cuts. I thought this durable cloth would be

The "natural man" with his rack of Hexentrics and Stopper clean climbing chocks. C. 1973.
Tom Frost

great for climbing. Ordering up some fabric, I had some knickers and double-seated shorts made. They sold well to our climbing friends, so I ordered some more.

Whenever we needed more corduroy, seven old men had to come out of retirement to crank up their machine at the mill. They warned us that when the hundreds of knife blades that cut the corduroy's wales got dull, it would be too expensive to sharpen them, and that would be the end of their machine.

Camping at a gaucho's *puesto*. Paso del Viento, Patagonia, Argentina. 1972. *Doug Tompkins*

As it turned out, we sold these knickers and shorts in small but steady numbers for ten years before the knives finally dulled and the loom was retired.

The next idea I had for clothing was the one that really took off. In the late sixties men did not wear bright, colorful clothes. "Active sportswear" consisted of your basic gray sweatshirt and pants, and the standard issue for climbing in Yosemite was tan cutoff chinos and white dress shirts bought from the thrift store. Then, on a winter climbing trip to Scotland in 1970, I bought

Drying out our inventory of rugby shirts and climbing ropes after a heavy rain flooded the basement of the old Hobson and Smith packinghouse. 1969. *Courtesy of Patagonia*

myself a regulation team rugby shirt to wear, thinking it would make a great shirt for rock climbing. Overbuilt to withstand the rigors of rugby, it had a collar that would keep the hardware slings from cutting into my neck. The basic color was blue, with two red and one yellow center stripe across the chest. Back in the States I wore it around climbing, and all my friends asked where they could get one.

We ordered a few shirts from Umbro, in England, and they sold straight off. We couldn't keep them in stock. Soon we began ordering shirts from New Zealand and Argentina as well. I began to see clothing as a way to help support the marginally profitable hardware business. At the time we had about 75 percent of the climbing hardware market, but we still weren't making much of a profit.

It was my second trip to Hong Kong. I was sitting in the little bar of the August Moon Hotel beating the heat with a San Miguel when the telex arrived. The Moon was a sleepy old dog of a place; they left you alone, so I liked it.

The bar was the only air-conditioned room in the place, and the room service beer was hotter than the tea, so I spent a lot of time there watching the good-luck koi gang drift around the aquarium.

We had started to make clothes because Yvon had some good ideas for rags and, let's face it, we were slowly going bust banging out bongs. I was working in a sweaty little plant on Stand Up Shorts, rugby shirts and climbing pants. Equipment for alpinists, as I saw it.

The girl put the telex down on the bar. It began to dissolve in the pool of water around the sweating glass. It could rot into the thick mahogany for all I cared. In production, all news is bad news; the telex was as welcome as a wart. Bracing myself with another round, I picked up the soggy dispatch and held it up to the fish tank.

It was from Vincent, our head peddler. He said a women's sportswear buyer had seen the clothes and wanted to know if we would make the Stand Up Shorts in women's sizing in a "non-ugly" color. I felt like I'd been cold-cocked with one of the koi. What the hell was sportswear, and what's so ugly about khaki? I asked for a glass of quinine water, figuring if it works for malaria, it'd work for sportswear.

Just me, the fish and the barkeep. My "equipment for alpinists" world was in pastel jeopardy. Was I going to have to wear argyle socks and strange shoes? Did the flattop have to go?

Maybe it was the beer; probably it was the handwriting on the wall. I saw the light. We were going to make clothes, some would call them sportswear. No matter; it was equipment to us. That's all we knew how to make.

Once past this semantic choke point, life's been good. I make equipment out of fabric and thread; I still have the flattop. Cotton, steel, rivet, or thread—it's all the same to me.

—Roger McDivitt
Patagonia Catalog, 1981

By 1972 we had taken over the abandoned meatpacking plant next door and begun to renovate its old offices as a retail store. We had added to our line polyurethane-coated rain *cagoules* and bivouac sacks from Scotland, boiled wool gloves and mittens from Austria, and hand-knit reversible "schizo" hats from Boulder. Plus Tom Frost had come up with some backpack designs, so we soon were running a full-on sewing operation in the loft above the old abattoir.

In the loft one day I decided to make myself a pair of bomber shorts, with a double seat that formed enormous back pockets. I made the patterns and cut the cloth. My foreman, Choong ok Sun Woo's bride, Young Sun, sewed them up out of number ten canvas duck, the fabric used for lawn furniture. To get the thread through, she had to use a walking foot machine, the one we used for sewing leather accessory patches on our packs. When she finished, she stood them on the table and laughed at the way they "stood up" all by themselves. But after hard use and about ten or twenty washings they were broken in and pretty comfortable. They soon became our second big clothing seller. We still make Stand Up Shorts but out of softer material.

While I began to get more ideas for clothing, Tom Frost and a climbing friend, Pete Carman, churned out more ideas for packs, including the first overnight wraparound internal frame pack for skiing and climbing, the Ultima Thule, and several heavy-duty rock-climbing packs (one made out of a tough fabric that smelled so odd we called it the Fish Pack). Our pack line soon earned a pan from *Backpacker* magazine, which found them too radical a departure from the Kelty-style frame packs of the time. The review ended with "How well would you expect ironmongers to sew?"* Perhaps we didn't know much about sewing, but we did know how to make things functional, tough, and simple—just as a good black-smith would. And while the packs never sold all that well, customers responded favorably to our simple "hand-forged" clothing.

*"Evaluations," *Backpacker Magazine*, Volume 5, 1974, p. 57

As we began to make more and more clothes (wool Chamonix guide sweaters, classic Mediterranean sailor shirts, canvas pants and shirts, and a technical line of rainwear—a predecessor to Gore-Tex—called Foamback), we needed to find a name for our clothing line. Chouinard was suggested at first. We already had a good image; why start from scratch? We had two reasons against it. First, we didn't want to dilute the image of Chouinard Equipment as a tool company by making clothing under that label. Second, we didn't want our clothes to be associated only with mountain climbing; we had a vision of a greater future than that.

The name Patagonia soon came up in our discussions. To most people, especially then, Patagonia was a name like Timbuktu or Shangri-la—far-off, interesting, not quite on the map. Patagonia brings to mind, as we once wrote in a catalog introduction, "romantic visions of glaciers tumbling into fjords, jagged windswept peaks, gauchos and condors." Our intent was to make clothing for those rugged southern Andes/Cape Horn conditions. It's been a good name for us, and it can be pronounced in every language.

To reinforce the tie to the real Patagonia, in 1973 we created a label with a stormy sky, jagged peaks based on the Mount Fitzroy skyline, and blue ocean.

One of the first products to bear the label nearly brought us to bankruptcy. The rugby shirt's sales had become a burgeoning underground fashion in the mountain shops. These stores shared our heritage; they had been started by climbers and backpackers who knew little about business but needed a way to support themselves. Originally they had found unexpected growth from the college fad of wearing Vibram-soled mountain boots to class and down jackets around the city. Now rugby shirts were bringing in new customers—only to be turned away because we couldn't supply the growing demand. In 1974 we made our big move and contracted directly with a garment factory in Hong Kong for three thousand shirts a month, in eight color combinations.

Where the inspiration for the label came from.
Mount Fitzroy peaks in Patagonia. *Barbara Rowell*

Business is growing!
Employees in 1974.
Tom Frost

It turned into a disaster. Shipments were late, and because the factory was accustomed to making trendy fashion clothing, the quality was terrible. They used too fine a thread, the shirts shrank horribly, and some even came in with three-quarter-length sleeves. We unloaded as many shirts as we could for less than cost and almost lost the company. Because we had been growing so quickly and were still not very profitable, we had severe cash-flow problems.

We knew how to keep inventory of our hard goods. We had steel bars and aluminum rod stock on the floor or in process and could just look into the finished bins to see how well stocked we were. What hardware we didn't make we imported from reliable sources, and Frost and I personally inspected every carabiner and chock for defects. But clothes were different. Fabric had to be ordered months ahead from sources and factories spread out all over the world; we could inspect for basic flaws, but not for colorfastness or shrinkage. We learned the hard way that there was a big difference between running a blacksmith shop and being in the rag business.

While the defective rugby shirts were emptying our account, Malinda and I had to endure endless boring lunches trying to convince bankers that we really didn't need any money, which was their bottom-line criterion for lending us some. One, a local farmers' bank, wouldn't lend to us because our inventory was scattered all over the world; the bankers wanted it all in one place (think silo!). At one point our accountant even introduced us to a Mafia connection in LA who wanted 28 percent interest. Malinda and I had never bought anything on credit, nor had the Frosts. The business had always paid its bills on time, and it killed us to put off payment to our suppliers. There were a lot of acid stomachs and sleepless nights for the Frosts and the Chouinards. The partnership strained to the breaking point, and we finally parted ways on the last day of 1975. The Frosts moved to Boulder, Colorado, to start a photographic equipment business, and Malinda and I were left the sole owners of a struggling climbing tool and clothing business.

With the Frosts gone, we replaced their chosen general manager with our own, and in 1979 Kris McDivitt took over the reins. Taking over the job at one of the many difficult times, she was a quick study. The company finally had a general manager who could fathom the mercurial creativity of the owners. Kris secured better financing, inspired the sales force, cajoled exclusive contracts from suppliers, mothered distraught employees, and used her flair for both intimacy and drama to mobilize the company into a cohesive whole. She also established and fiercely protected Patagonia's image through close oversight of the design and art departments. We had a great partnership, in that no matter how crazy an idea I'd come up with, it was not crazy to her—until proved to be unrealistic. She was a great people person who was able to communicate to everyone why he or she had to take some of my more radical ideas seriously or at least humor me until I forgot about them.

In an interview a few years ago Kris recalled the state of the company and showed why we were right in trusting her at the helm:

"There were only five of us in the company in 1972. In 1977, there were 16 of us and my brother was general manager. In 1979, my brother quit and Yvon didn't want to run the company—he wanted to climb and surf and all those things.

"So he gave me the companies, saying in effect, 'Here's Patagonia. Here's Chouinard Equipment. Do with them what you will. I'm going climbing.'

"I had no business experience so I started asking people for free advice. I just called up presidents of banks and said, 'I've been given these companies to run and I've no idea what I'm doing. I think someone should help me.'

"And they did. If you just ask people for help—if you just admit that you don't know something—they will fall all over themselves trying to help. So, from there I began building the company. I was really the translator for Yvon's vision and aims for the company."

I had always avoided thinking of myself as a businessman. I was a climber, a

Kristine McDivitt, general manager and CEO of Patagonia for thirteen years.
Surfers Point, Ventura, 1985. *Courtesy of Patagonia.*

surfer, a kayaker, a skier, and a blacksmith. We simply enjoyed making good tools and functional clothes that we, and our friends, wanted. Malinda's and my only personal assets were a beat-up Ford van and a heavily mortgaged soon-to-be-condemned cabin on the beach. Now we had a heavily leveraged company with employees with families of their own, all depending on our being successful.

After we had pondered our responsibilities and financial liabilities, one day it dawned on me that I *was* a businessman and would probably be one for a long time. It was also clear that in order to survive at this game, we had to get serious. I also knew that I would never be happy playing by the normal rules of business; I wanted to distance myself as far as possible from those pasty-faced corpses in suits I saw in airline magazine ads. If I had to be a businessman, I was going to do it on my own terms.

One of my favorite sayings about entrepreneurship is: If you want to understand the entrepreneur, study the juvenile delinquent. The delinquent is saying with his actions, "This sucks. I'm going to do my own thing." Since I had never wanted to be a businessman, I needed a few good reasons to be one. One thing I did not want to change, even if we got serious: Work had to be enjoyable on a daily basis. We all had to come to work on the balls of our feet and go up the stairs two steps at a time. We needed to be surrounded by friends who could dress whatever way they wanted, even be barefoot. We all needed to have flextime to surf the waves when they were good, or ski the powder after a big snowstorm, or stay home and take care of a sick child. We needed to blur that distinction between work and play and family.

Breaking the rules and making my own system work are the creative part of management that is particularly satisfying for me. But I don't jump into things without doing my homework.

For instance, in 1978 I wrote a book on ice-climbing techniques that had taken me twelve years to write because I had to travel, climb, and study snow and ice climbing in every major country that practiced alpine climbing, trying to come up with a unified technique for my book *Climbing Ice*. In the introduction I wrote:

> Until the 1970s the countries in the world where snow and ice climbing was practiced were divided into those that used only flat-footed (or French) cramponing techniques and those that climbed on the front points of the crampons. Both schools of climbing were equally proficient, but neither side was willing to admit the worth of the other's technique. It is possible to do all your ice climbing with only one technique—as many persons still do—but it is not the most efficient way nor does it make for a very interesting experience. It is like knowing only one dance. When the music changes, you are still dancing, but rather out of tune. So, as is usually the case in these matters, the truth lies right down the middle. Now all the best ice climbers know and apply both methods in their cramponing.

I did the same thing in my search for business knowledge. Over the next few years I read every book of business, searching for a philosophy that would work for us. I was especially interested in books on Japanese or Scandinavian styles of management because I knew the American way of doing business offered only one of many possible routes.

I didn't find any American company we could use as a role model. Either it was too large and conservative for us to relate to, or it didn't have the same values. However, there was one company, Esprit, owned by my friends Doug and Susie Tompkins, that was contrary and that shared our values. Doug was a climbing and surfing friend who in the early sixties started The North Face store in San Francisco. We linked up when he did the wholesale distribution of my hardware in 1964–65. He was the one who introduced me to the remote region of Chile and Argentina called Patagonia in 1968, after he had sold The North Face, and in fact it was while we were on that trip that Susie and a friend started the business Plain Jane, which became Esprit. Doug also had a visceral dislike for authority and always relished breaking the rules. Esprit was a much larger company than we were and had already encountered and solved many of the problems of growth, so they were a tremendous help to us in the early years.

Doug Tompkins, with Royal Robbins, Reg Lake, and others, introduced me to white-water kayaking. We called ourselves the Do Boys, a takeoff on the awkward Japanese translation of *active sports* to *do sports*. My first time out with them in the southern Sierras turned out to be the usual "sandbag." On my first day of kayaking, we ran a Class 3 section of the Stanislaus River, the second day a Class 4 section of the Lower Merced, the third day a Class 5 stretch of the Tuolomne. And so it went for twelve days. When it was over, I had fifteen stitches in my face, and my back was so bad off I had to pick up a hitchhiker to drive me home. That was the usual way you learned to do risk sports in those days, before there were guides, outdoor schools, and instruction books.

I've always thought of myself as an 80 percenter. I like to throw myself passion-

Doug Tompkins, left, and Royal Robbins. *Courtesy of Patagonia*

Some of the Do Boys after the three-day first descent of the Clarks Fork of the Yellowstone River. Doug Tompkins, Rob Lessor, John Wasson, Y.C., and Reg Lake. 1986. *Doug Tompkins*

ately into a sport or activity until I reach about an 80 percent proficiency level. To go beyond that requires an obsession and degree of specialization that doesn't appeal to me. Once I reach that 80 percent level I like to go off and do something totally different; that probably explains the diversity of the Patagonia product line—and why our versatile, multifaceted clothes are the most successful.

Multifunctional technical clothing became our new focus once we survived our first major cash-flow crisis (by finally securing a line of revolving credit with a bank). Our first technical product had been the Foamback jacket, an advance over the polyurethane rainwear of the time, which condensed badly on the inside. We applied a thin layer of foam and a scrim to the inside of the nylon shell, which added warmth and reduced condensation. The design work led us to tackle the larger problem of how to dress for the high mountains, where unpredictable weather can be life-threatening.

Tom Brokaw on Mount Rainier, Washington.
Rick Ridgeway

At a time when the entire mountaineering community relied on the traditional, moisture-absorbing layers of cotton, wool, and down, we looked elsewhere for inspiration—and protection. We decided that a staple of North Atlantic fishermen, the synthetic pile sweater, would make an ideal mountain sweater because it insulated well without absorbing moisture.

We needed to find some fabric to test out our idea, and it wasn't easy to find. Finally, in 1976, Malinda, acting on a hunch, drove to the California Merchandise Mart in Los Angeles. She found what she was looking for at Malden Mills, freshly emerged from bankruptcy after the collapse of the fake fur coat market and selling off its stock of fabrics. We sewed a few sweaters and field-tested them in alpine conditions. The polyester fabric was astonishingly warm, particularly when used with a shell. It insulated when wet but also dried in minutes, and it reduced the number of layers a climber had to wear. Our first pile garments, stiff with their sizing treatment, were made from fabric intended for toilet seat covers.

We couldn't muster an order large enough to have the fabric customized, so we had to use Malden's existing stock, which came in an ugly tan and equally hideous powder blue. When we exhibited the jackets at a trade show in Chicago, one buyer, fingering a jacket, asked our salesman, Tex Bossier, what kind of fur it was made of. "It's rare Siberian blue poodle fur, ma'am," Tex deadpanned. Ugly as they were, and they pilled like crazy once in use, the pile jacket soon became an outdoor staple.

It does no good, though, to wear a quick-drying insulation layer over cotton underwear, which absorbs body moisture and then freezes. So in 1980 we came out with insulating long underwear made of polypropylene, a synthetic fiber that has a very low specific gravity and absorbs no water. It had been used in the manufacture of industrial commodities like marine ropes, which float. Its first adaptation to clothing was as a nonwoven lining in disposable diapers, where the wicking ability of the fiber kept the baby dry by carrying the moisture away from the skin and transferring it to the more absorbent material in the diaper's outer layers.

A Norwegian company had already developed a thin stretch-knit underwear of polypropylene that wicked perspiration from the skin, but it had one major limitation: It was so thin and porous it provided little insulation. Our knit fabric was four times thicker, since it was brushed on the inside to achieve extra loft and softness.

Using the capabilities of this new underwear as the basis of a system, we became the first company to teach the outdoor community, through essays in our catalog, the concept of layering. This approach involves wearing an inner layer against the skin for moisture transport, a middle layer of pile for insulation, and then an outer shell layer for wind and moisture protection.

Our teaching paid off. Before long we saw much less cotton and wool in the mountains—and a lot of pilled powder blue and tan pile sweaters worn over striped polypropylene underwear.

But polypropylene, like pile, had its problems. It had a very low melting temperature, and customers were melting their underwear in commercial Laundromat dryers, which are often much hotter than home dryers. Also, polypropylene is hydrophobic and repels water, so it was difficult to get thoroughly clean and thus retained odors. It also turned out that its wicking properties were not inherent in the fabric but the result of oils applied in the process of spinning and knitting that, after twenty washings or so, wore off.

Although both pile and polypropylene were immediately successful, and we did not yet have significant competition, we worked hard from the start to improve their quality and overcome the problems of both fabrics.

Improving pile was a gradual process. We worked closely with Malden to develop first a soft bunting fabric, an imitation wool that pilled less, and eventually Synchilla, an even softer double-faced fabric that did not pill at all. With Synchilla, we learned an important lesson in business. While Malden Mills' easier access to financial capital made many of the innovations possible, the fabric would never have been developed if we had not actively shaped the research and

One of my favorite image
photos of pile in use.
Gary Bingham

development process. From that point forward,
we began to make significant investments in
our own research and design departments. Our
fabric lab and our fabric development departments, in particular, became the envy
of the industry. Mills were anxious to work with us on developing projects,

because they knew that if Patagonia helped them, the developed fabric would likely be a better one.

Our replacement for polypropylene, the same year we developed Synchilla, did not come from a mutual development process with a mill; it came from out of the blue. Sometimes good ideas spring from having a sense of where you want to go, of having a vision of the next level of products. In 1984 I was walking around the sporting goods show in Chicago when I saw a demonstration of some polyester football jerseys being cleaned of grass stains. Synthetic fibers, like polypropylene and polyester, are made of plastic resins that are extruded through a die to create a thin, round fiber. These plastic fibers are very smooth, and clothing woven from them is difficult to clean because the slick fibers repel the soap and water of normal washing.

The company that made the football jerseys, Milliken, had developed a process that permanently etched the surface of the fiber so that the surface was hydrophilic—water-loving. You can easily understand the difference between the two kinds of polyester fibers by dropping a bit of water on glass. On smooth glass it stays as a drop, but if you do the same on a piece of etched glass, the drop spreads out.

Forget about the football jerseys, I thought. Here is the perfect fiber for underwear! Polyester had a much higher melting temperature, so it would be safe in clothes dryers, and etching made the fiber wick like crazy, yet it didn't absorb and hold water inside the fiber, so was quick-drying.

Our more conservative employees wanted us to phase in the new material slowly, especially because we were introducing Synchilla at the same time. Together polypropylene and bunting fleece represented 70 percent of our sales. Yet you can't wait until you have all the answers before you act. It's often a greater risk to phase in products because you lose the advantage of being first with a new idea.

I had faith that the product was good, and I knew the market, so we forged ahead to shift our entire line of polypropylene underwear to the new Capilene polyester. Our loyal core customers quickly realized the advantages of Capilene and Synchilla, and our sales soared. Other companies, just introducing ripoffs of our bunting and polypropylene clothes, had to scramble to keep up.

The competition always stayed close on our heels, but we managed to keep innovating and improving our products. In the early 1980s we made another important shift. At a time when all outdoor products were tan, forest green, or, at the most colorful, rust, we drenched the Patagonia line in vivid color. We introduced cobalt, teal, French red, mango, seafoam, and iced mocha. Patagonia clothing, still rugged, moved beyond bland-looking to blasphemous. And it worked. The rest of the industry spent the better part of a decade catching up.

The runaway popularity of dramatic colors and the growing appeal of technical fabrics like Synchilla created a dramatic shift in our fortunes. The Patagonia label had now become as much of a fad as the rugby shirt, and our popularity extended well beyond the outdoor community to fashion consumers. Although we devoted most of our selling efforts and catalog space to explaining the technical merits of layered clothing for hard-core enthusiasts, the best-selling pieces were our least technical: Baggies beach shorts and shelled Synchilla bomber-style jackets.

From the mid-1980s to 1990 sales grew from twenty million to one hundred million dollars. Malinda and I were not personally any wealthier because we kept the profits in the company. In many ways, the growth was exciting. We were certainly never bored. New employees, including those in the lowest-paid positions in retail stores or the warehouse, could rise rapidly to better-paying jobs. For a few positions we conducted searches, and we could claim our pick of the litter within both the apparel and outdoor industries. But most of the new employees we hired came through a well-rooted and fast-growing grapevine. When a new job opened up, our employees let their friends know about it, and then friends of friends, and relatives.

Despite our own growth at Patagonia, we were able, in many ways, to keep alive our cultural values as we grew. We still came to work on the balls of our feet.

We were surrounded by friends who could dress however they wanted. People ran or surfed at lunch or played volleyball in the sandpit at the back of the building. The company sponsored ski and climbing trips, and many more trips were undertaken informally by groups of friends who would drive up to the Sierras on Friday night and arrive home, groggy but happy, in time for work on Monday morning.

Our expansion necessitated some changes. In 1984 we changed the name of Great Pacific Iron Works to Lost Arrow Corporation, as the parent holding company for the other operations: Patagonia, Inc. designed, manufactured, and distributed the clothing; Chouinard Equipment did the same for hard goods. We formed a new Great Pacific Iron Works to run the retail stores, and Patagonia Mail Order, Inc. became a separate entity. That year we built a new Lost Arrow administration building that had no private offices, even for the executives. This

Great Pacific Child Development kids off on a discovery trip. *Courtesy of Patagonia*

architectural arrangement sometimes created distractions but helped keep communication open. Management worked together in a large open area that employees quickly dubbed the corral. We provided a cafeteria that served healthy, mostly vegetarian food where employees could gather throughout the day. And we opened, at Malinda's insistence, an on-site child care center, Great Pacific Child Development Center, Inc. At the time it was one of only 150 in the country; today there are more than 3,000. The presence of children playing in the yard or having lunch with their mothers and fathers in the cafeteria helped keep the company atmosphere more familial than corporate. We also offered, mostly for the benefit of new parents but also for other employees, flexible working hours and job sharing.

We never had to make a break from the traditional corporate culture that makes businesses hidebound and inhibits creativity. For the most part, we simply made the effort to hold to our own particular tradition. At one time

MALINDA'S VIEW OF CHILD CARE

It didn't start out by careful design. Even though my minor was in home economics, I was one of the few to graduate completely devoid of any classes in preschool training. The real root of our day care center was that the Frosts brought their babies to work, so we did too. As we hired new employees, they followed suit. Baby beds were draped over computer monitors, to the horror of those who understood computers, but it wasn't until the arrival of one baby, born a screamer, that we realized the havoc the babies created in the workplace. The baby's mother took to sitting in the car outside with the colicky infant, and we all felt guilty.

The idea of devoting either cash or space, both in short supply, to infants was debated for two more years. We had no idea how to start a day care center, but several parents pushed ahead with the idea. Long after it was opened, we learned that it was a radical idea, one fraught with laws and hysterical parents. Only after we found Anita Garaway Furtaw, nationally recognized in child development, did we relax. She helped formulate the state and national laws and standards we now accept as routine in the family workplace.

Anita also tipped us into an even larger social revolution, maternity leave. As mother after mother began arriving from the delivery room with their damp new-borns, Anita declared her staff was in open rebellion. The parents replied in kind when I naively announced they couldn't bring babies in until they were at least eight weeks old. "How will we eat or pay our mortgages?" they cried, and threatened to quit.

No child care discussion starts without high drama. We agreed to pay them to stay home and nurse their infants, sweetening the pot by telling them the fathers could have leave too. As the years roll by and some of our original day care kids have become parents and employees, our policies have become federal law—in no small part through Anita's lobbying.

—Y.C.

Lunchtime in the babies' room. *Courtesy of Patagonia*

that tradition looked peculiar, but it no longer does. Many American industries have adopted more casual workplaces, and we played a role in starting that trend.

In growing the business, however, we used traditional textbook practices—increasing the number of products, opening new dealers and new stores of our own, developing new foreign markets—and soon we were in serious danger of outgrowing our breeches. We had nearly outgrown our natural niche, the specialty outdoor market. By the late 1980s the company was growing at a rate that, if sustained, would have made us a billion-dollar company in a decade. To reach that theoretical billion-dollar mark, we would have to begin selling to mass merchants or department stores. This challenged the basic design principles we had established for ourselves as the makers of the best hardware. Can a company that wants to make the best-quality outdoor clothing in the world be the size of Nike? Can a ten-table, three-star French restaurant retain its third star when it adds fifty tables? Can you have it all? The question haunted me throughout the 1980s as Patagonia evolved. Another problem came to haunt me more: the deterioration of the natural world. I saw that deterioration first with my own eyes when I returned to climb or surf or fish in places I knew, like Nepal, Africa, and Polynesia, and saw what had happened in the few years since I'd last been there.

I continued to practice my MBA theory of management, management by absence, while I wear-tested our clothing and equipment in the most extreme conditions of the Himalayas and South America. I was the outside guy, responsible for bringing back new ideas. A company needs someone to go out and get the temperature of the world, so for years I would come home excited about ideas for products, new markets, or new materials. Then I began to see rapid changes in the world, and more and more I came home with stories of environmental and social devastation.

In Africa, forests and grassland were disappearing as the populations grew. Global warming was melting glaciers that had been part of the continent's climbing history. The emergence of AIDS and Ebola coincided with the clear-cutting of forests and the wholesale pursuit of bush meat, such as infected chimpanzees.

On a kayaking trip to the Russian Far East, before the collapse of the Soviet Union, I found that the Russians had destroyed much of their country trying to keep up with the United States in their arms race. Their oil, mineral, and timber extraction had devastated the land, and failed industrial efforts had contaminated cities and farmlands. They were eating their seed corn.

Closer to home, I saw the relentless paving over of Southern California's remaining coastline and hillsides. In Wyoming, where I had spent summers for thirty years, I saw fewer wild animals each year, caught smaller fish, and suffered through weeks of debilitating, record-setting ninety-degree heat. But most environmental devastation the eye doesn't see. I learned more by reading about the rapid loss of topsoil and groundwater, about the clear-cutting of tropical forests and the growing list of endangered plant and animal and bird species, and about people in the once-pristine Arctic who are now being warned not to eat local mammals and fish because of toxins from industrial nations.

At the same time, we slowly became aware that uphill battles fought by small, dedicated groups of people to save patches of habitat could yield significant results. The first lesson had come right here at home, in the early seventies. A group of us had gone to our local theater to watch a surf movie. At the end a young surfer asked the audience to attend a city council meeting to speak out against the city's plan to channel and develop the mouth of the Ventura River, one of the best surf points in the area and only five hundred yards from Patagonia's offices.

Several of us went to the meeting to protest against the possible destruction of our surf break. We knew vaguely that the Ventura River had once been a major

Local boys with steelhead from the Ventura River. 1920.
Courtesy of Patagonia

habitat for steelhead. In fact, in the 1940s the river had an annual run of four to five thousand sea-run rainbows. Then two dams were built, and the water was diverted. Except for winter rains, the only water left at the river mouth flowed from the sewage treatment plant. At the city council meeting, several experts testified that the river was dead and that channeling would have no effect on remaining birds or other wildlife or on the surf break.

Then Mark Capelli, a young graduate student, gave a slide show of photos he had taken along the river—of the birds that lived in the willows, of the muskrats and water snakes, of eels that spawned in the estuary. When he showed a slide of a steelhead smolt, everyone stood up and cheered. Yes, several dozen steelhead still came to spawn in our "dead" river.

The development plan was defeated. We gave Mark office space, a mailbox, and small contributions to help him fight the battle for the river. As more development plans cropped up, the Friends of the Ventura River worked to defeat them and to clean up the water and to increase its flow. Wildlife increased, and a few more steelhead began to spawn. Mark taught us two important lessons: A grassroots effort could make a difference, and degraded habitat could, with effort, be restored. Inspired by his work, we began to make regular donations to smaller groups working to save or restore habitat, rather than give the money to large NGOs (nongovernmental organizations) with big staffs, overheads, and corporate connections. In 1986 we committed ourselves to donate 10 percent of profits each year to these groups. We later upped the ante to 1 percent of sales, or 10 percent of pretax profits, whichever was greater. We have kept that commitment every year, boom or bust.

In 1988 we initiated our first national environmental campaign, supporting an alternative master plan to deurbanize the Yosemite Valley. We solicited essays from writers and then printed them in the catalog and devoted display space in our stores. As we became more and more involved, we waged campaigns on behalf of salmon and river restoration, against GATT and "free trade" agreements and genetically modified organisms (GMOs), for the Wildlands Project, and, in Europe, against heavy truck traffic through the Alps.

We also realized that in addition to addressing these external crises, we had to look within the company and reduce our own role as a corporate polluter. We began recycling paper waste in 1984 and conducted an intensive search for a source of paper with a higher percentage of recycled content for our catalog. Since we were the first catalog in the United States to use recycled paper, the result was

What does an outdoor clothing company know about genetically engineered food?

Not enough, and neither do you.

Even the scientists working on genetic engineering admit they don't know the full story. But despite the fact that we know so little about the impacts, a salmon has already been engineered that grows at twice the rate of normal salmon, a strain of corn has been created with pesticide in every cell, and trees have been engineered with less lignin to break down more easily in the pulping process. What will be the impact on our health, and the health of the ecosystem, once these new species make it out into the wild or into our food supply? No one knows.

Let's not repeat the mistakes we've made in the past with such inadequately tested technologies as DDT and nuclear energy. We don't know enough about the dangers of genetic engineering. Let's find out all the risks before we turn genetically modified organisms loose on the world, or continue to eat them in our food.

Find out more at
www.patagonia.com/enviroaction

patagonia®

Photo: Jim Arneson © 2001 Patagonia, Inc.

a disaster the first season. The still-experimental paper did not hold the ink very well; the photos were blurry and the colors "muddy." But in that first year alone our switching to recycled paper saved 3.5 million kilowatt-hours of electricity and 6 million gallons of water; kept 52,000 pounds of pollutants out of the air and 1,560 cubic yards of solid waste out of landfills, and prevented 14,500 trees from being felled. The next year the quality of the paper was vastly improved. We also researched and pioneered the use of recycled, reused, and less toxic materials in our construction and remodeling projects. We worked with Wellman and Malden Mills to develop recycled polyester for use in our Synchilla fleece.

All the while we continued to grow. We experienced so much success on so many fronts during the late 1980s that we began to believe the expansion would never end. And we planned to just keep going.

Not that it was a cakewalk. We struggled to support that rapid growth rate. We constantly outgrew our offices, as well as the capabilities of our suppliers, bankers, internal information systems, and managers. It seemed that every couple of years we had to buy a bigger, more powerful computer. I don't use computers even now and have no interest in any electronic stuff, but one day I thought I should at least go over to the computer room and check out the new IBM System 38 that everyone was calling Roscoe. I looked at this big metal thing and exclaimed, "I paid a quarter of a million dollars for that!"

"No," the manager said, "that's the air conditioner. Roscoe is over there."

Malinda and I often argued with our managers for more restrained, or "natural," growth, especially in wholesale. But we pressed those same managers to expand retail and mail order in pursuit of more direct customer relationships and to develop an international business that could help provide balance during weak domestic seasons. We also pushed for new sport-specific product lines, and by 1989 we were offering technical shells for mountaineering, skiing, paddling, fishing, and sailing, as well as insulation and underwear for all outdoor activities. All

the same, the growth came primarily from less technical sportswear, and much of it through wholesale. New sport-specific product lines were plagued by problems with quality, delivery, and sales. Overall, product incubation time had slowed from one year to two.

Our first big company crisis came not from a sales crunch but from legal trouble. In the late 1980s Chouinard Equipment, which we still owned, became the target of several lawsuits. None involved faulty equipment or climbers. We were sued by a window washer, a plumber, a stagehand, and someone who broke his ankle in a tug-of-war contest using our climbing ropes. The basis of each suit was improper warning: that we had failed to properly warn these customers about the dangers inherent in using our equipment for uses we could not predict. Then came a more serious suit, from the family of a lawyer who was killed when he incorrectly tied into one of our harnesses in a beginning climbing class.

The litigators thought that Chouinard Equipment and Patagonia were the same company and since Patagonia was doing so well, they could milk the corporation. Our insurance company refused to fight any of the suits and settled out of court. Our insurance premiums went up 2,000 percent in one year. Eventually Chouinard Equipment Ltd. filed for Chapter 11, a move that gave the employees time to gather capital for a buyout. They successfully purchased the assets, moved the company to Salt Lake City, and built their own company, Black Diamond Ltd., that to this day continues to make the world's best climbing and backcountry ski gear.

From 1985 to 1990 we made some of the finest foul-weather clothing for serious sailing but failed to make it a viable business. The wholesale model didn't work because the typical hardware chandleries were resistant to selling clothing. We then tried direct mail order with a sailing-specific catalog. We finally realized that there were very few serious sailors, and the weekend sailor had no need for expensive foul-weather gear. The sailing line fell victim to our belt tightening in 1991. *Onne van der Wal*

When we weren't dealing with lawsuits, our international business provided sleepless nights. We got off to a rocky and loss-plagued start in Europe. Relationships with licensees and distributors failed, and so did the first managers of our own operations in Europe and Japan. Kris McDivitt saw the operations of the company were getting increasingly technical and thought we needed a real CEO with more business experience, so we hired one, and she continued to manage our brand and image.

We decided that a retail presence in key cities or recreational areas was essential to getting our full story across to the customer, both abroad and at home. We opened our first European store in Chamonix, France, the home base of the Alpine climbing world, in 1987, and a store in Tokyo in 1989. We opened new domestic stores at a steady pace—two per year after 1986, when we first ventured beyond Ventura to open a shop in San Francisco. Most of our stores were successful from the start.

Patagonia Mail Order had more difficulty, mostly because we rejected the traditional industry strategies of renting mailing lists and sending out "new" catalogs to the same people when only the cover had changed. We operated within these constraints for most of a decade without identifying effective alternatives. We also suffered from not knowing how to manage mail-order inventory effectively. This led to hoarding until the season's end, then funneling the overbuy back to the wholesale division, which had to dump the goods at increasingly larger annual yard sales.

Wholesale did manage to avoid some of the worst excesses common to that business channel. We declined to sell to the department stores and sporting goods chains that knocked at our doors. We cut our dealer base by half, increasing our commitment to the most engaged and loyal dealers. But wholesale still relied on growth from a limited, mostly "nontechnical" part of the line. It was difficult to sell our clothes for paddling, sailing, and fly-fishing because we were competing with well-established specialty companies. We worried that our image might become too soft and sportswear-oriented.

To re-create the entrepreneurial atmosphere of the sort we'd had at Chouinard Equipment, we broke the line into eight categories and hired eight product czars to manage them. Each was responsible for his or her own product development, marketing, inventory, quality control, and coordination with the three sales channels—wholesale, mail order, and retail. In 1990 we geared our financing and production plans for another year of 40 percent growth. We added another hundred people to our staff in advance of this growth to avoid having to play catch-up later. To make room for them, we built out part of the old slaughterhouse.

Looking back now, I see that we made all the classic mistakes of a growing company. We failed to provide the proper training for the new company leaders, and the strain of managing a company with eight autonomous product divisions and

Shooting line at Lago Fagnano. Tierra del Fuego, Argentina.
Don't try this with dentures! *Doug Tompkins*

three channels of distribution exceeded management's skills. We never developed the mechanisms to encourage them to work together in ways that kept the overall business objectives in sight.

Several planning efforts had to be aborted; no one could solve the Rubik's cube of matching market-specific product development with such a complex distribution mix. Organization charts looked like the Sunday crossword puzzle and were issued almost as frequently. The company was restructured five times in five years; no plan worked better than the last one.

At one point we decided we needed another perspective, and Malinda and I, along with our CEO and CFO, sought the advice of a well-regarded consultant. We contacted Dr. Michael Kami, who had run strategic planning for IBM and, at some point, had turned Harley-Davidson around. We all flew to Florida to see him. Dr. Kami was a small man in his seventies with a squeaky, heavily accented voice, a full beard, and a lot of restless energy. He lived on an enormous yacht and wore a captain's cap and an open shirt with epaulets.

Before he could help us, he said, he wanted to know why we were in business. I told him the history of the company and how I considered myself a craftsman who had just happened to grow a successful business. I told him I'd always had a dream that when I had enough money, I'd sail off to the South Seas looking for the perfect wave and the ultimate bonefish flat. We told him the reason we hadn't sold out and retired was that we were pessimistic about the fate of the world and felt a responsibility to use our resources to do something about it. We told him about our tithing program, how we had given away a million dollars just in the past year to over two hundred organizations, and that our bottom-line reason for staying in the business was to make money we could give away.

Dr. Kami thought for a while and then said, "I think that's bullshit. If you're really serious about giving money away, you'd sell the company for a hundred million or so, keep a couple million for yourselves, and put the rest in a foundation. That way you could invest the principal and give away six or eight million dollars every year. And, if you sold to the right buyer, they would probably continue your tithing program because it's good advertising."

My managers protested.

"What are *you* worried about?" Dr. Kami said, turning to them. "You're young. You'll find other jobs!"

I said I was worried about what would happen to the company if I sold out.

"So maybe you're kidding yourself," he said, "about why you're in business."

It was as if the Zen master had hit us over the head with a stick, but instead of finding enlightenment we walked away more confused than ever.

I was still wondering why I was *really* in business when, in 1991, after all those years of 30 percent to 50 percent compound annual growth and trying to have it all, Patagonia hit the wall. The country had entered a recession, and the growth we had always planned on, and bought inventory for, stopped. Our sales crunch came not from a decline from the previous year, but from a "mere" 20 percent increase! Nevertheless, the 20 percent shortfall nearly did us in. Dealers canceled orders, and inventory began to build. Neither the mail order nor the international division could meet its forecasts, and both returned inventory as well. We cut back production as much as we could for spring and fall. We froze hiring and nonessential travel. We dropped new products and discontinued marginal sellers.

The crisis soon deepened. Our primary lender, Security Pacific Bank, was itself in financial trouble, and it sharply reduced our credit line—twice within several months. To bring our borrowing within the new limits, we had to reduce spending drastically. We made plans to shut down our offices and sales showrooms in London, Vancouver, and Munich. We let go our CEO and CFO and returned Kris McDivitt as our CEO. We brought in our European manager, Alain Devoldere, to act temporarily as chief operating officer.

We had never laid people off simply to reduce overhead. In fact we had never laid anyone off for any reason. Not only was the company like an extended family, but for many it *was* a family, because we had always hired friends, friends of

Patagonia walkabout in Patagonia.
1991. *Courtesy of Patagonia*

friends, and their relatives. Husbands and wives, mothers and sons, brothers and sisters, and cousins and in-laws worked together or in different departments. Layoffs are not a pleasant prospect for any company, but for us the idea was almost unthinkable, and the tension became, as layoffs became more likely, nearly unbearable.

We considered such alternatives as pay cuts and reduced hours, but in the end we decided that only layoffs would solve the problem we had created; in ramping up, we had added too many people to do what was now too little work. On July 31,

1991, Black Wednesday, we let go 120 employees—20 percent of the workforce. That was certainly the single darkest day of the company's history.

I realized that our crisis was a microcosm of what was going on all over the world. The World Watch Institute's state of the world report for that year, 1991, stated: "With an annual output of $20 trillion, the global economy now produces in 17 days what it took an entire year to generate in 1900. Already, economic activity has breached numerous local, regional, and global thresholds, resulting in the spread of deserts, acidification of lakes and forests, and the buildup of greenhouse gases. If growth proceeds along the lines of recent decades, it is only a matter of time before global systems collapse under the pressure."

Our own company had exceeded its resources and limitations; we had become dependent, like the world economy, on growth we could not sustain. But as a small company we couldn't ignore the problem and wish it away. We were forced to rethink our priorities and institute new practices. We had to start breaking the rules.

I took a dozen of my top managers to Argentina, to the windswept mountains of the real Patagonia, for a walkabout. In the course of roaming around those wildlands, we asked ourselves why we were in business and what kind of business we wanted Patagonia to be. A billion-dollar company? Okay, but not if it meant we had to make products we couldn't be proud of. We also discussed what we could do to help stem the environmental harm we caused as a company. We talked about the values we had in common and the shared culture that had brought everyone to Patagonia, Inc. and not to another company.

When we returned, we put together our first board of directors, made up of trusted friends and advisers. One of them was author and deep ecologist Jerry Mander. At one of our board meetings, when we were struggling to put into words our values and our mission statement, Jerry skipped lunch and went off by himself. He returned with a perfectly crafted article.

This is what Jerry Mander presented to the board that day:

OUR VALUES

We begin with the premise that all life on Earth is facing a critical time, during which survivability will be the issue that increasingly dominates public concern. Where survivability is not the issue, the quality of human experience of life may be, as well as the decline in health of the natural world as reflected in the loss of biodiversity, cultural diversity, and the planet's life support systems.

The root causes of this situation include basic values embodied in our economic system, including the values of the corporate world. Primary among the problematic corporate values are the primacy of expansion and short-term profit over such other considerations as quality, sustainability, environmental and human health, and successful communities.

The fundamental goal of this corporation is to operate in such a manner that we are fully aware of the above conditions, and attempt to re-order the hierarchy of corporate values, while producing products that enhance both human and environmental conditions.

To help achieve these changes, we will make our operating decisions based on the following list of values. They are not presented in order of importance. All are equally important. They represent an "ecology" of values that must be emphasized in economic activity that can mitigate the environmental and social crisis of our times.

- All decisions of the company are made in the context of the environmental crisis. We must strive to do no harm. Wherever possible, our acts should serve to decrease the problem. Our activities in this area will be under constant evaluation and re-assessment as we seek constant improvement.
- Maximum attention is given to product quality, as defined by durability, minimum use of natural resources (including materials, raw energy, and transport), multi-functionalism, non-obsolescence, and the kind of

beauty that emerges from absolute suitability to task. Concern over transitory fashion trends is specifically *not* a corporate value.

- The board and management recognize that successful communities are part of a sustainable environment. We consider ourselves to be an integral part of communities that also include our employees, the communities in which we live, our suppliers and customers. We recognize our responsibilities to all these relationships and make our decisions with their general benefit in mind. It is our policy to employ people who share the fundamental values of this corporation, while representing cultural and ethnic diversity.

- Without giving its achievement primacy, we seek to profit on our activities. However, growth and expansion are values *not* basic to this corporation.

- To help mitigate any negative environmental consequences of our business activity, we impose on ourselves an annual tax of one percent of our gross sales, or ten percent of profits, whichever is greater. All proceeds of this tax are granted to local community and environmental activism.

- At all levels of operation—board, management, and staff—Patagonia encourages pro-active stances that reflect our values. These include activities that influence the larger corporate community to also adjust its values and behavior, and that support, through activism and financially, grassroots and national campaigners who work to solve the current environmental and social crisis.

- In our internal operations, top management will work as a group, and with maximum transparency. This includes an "open book" policy that enables employees easy access to decisions, within normal boundaries of personal privacy and "trade secrecy." At all levels of corporate activity, we encourage open communications, a collaborative atmosphere and maximum simplicity, while we simultaneously seek dynamism and innovation.

—Y.C.

We knew that uncontrolled growth put at risk the values that had made the company succeed so far. Those values couldn't be expressed in a how-to operations manual that offers pat answers. We needed philosophical and inspirational guides to make sure we always asked the right questions and found the right answers. We spoke of these guides as philosophies, one for each of our major departments and functions.

While my managers debated what steps to take to address the sales and cash-flow crisis, I began to lead weeklong employee seminars in these newly written philosophies. We'd take a busload at a time to places like Yosemite or the Marin Headlands above San Francisco, camp out, and gather under the trees to talk. The goal was to teach every employee in the company our business and environmental ethics and values. When money finally got so tight we couldn't afford even to hire buses, we camped in the local Los Padres National Forest, but we kept training.

I realize now that what I was trying to do was to instill in my company, at a critical time, lessons that I had already learned as an individual and as a climber, surfer, kayaker, and fly fisherman. I had always tried to live my own life fairly simply, and by 1991, knowing what I knew about the state of the environment, I had begun to eat lower on the food chain and reduce my consumption of material goods. Doing risk sports had taught me another important lesson: Never exceed your limits. You push the envelope, and you live for those moments when you're right on the edge, but you don't go over. You have to be true to yourself; you have to know your strengths and limitations and live within your means. The same is true for a business. The sooner a company tries to be what it is not, the sooner it tries to "have it all," the sooner it will die.

I've been a student of Zen philosophy for many years. In Zen archery, for example, you forget about the goal—hitting the bull's-eye—and instead focus on all the individual movements involved in shooting an arrow. You practice your stance, reaching back and smoothly pulling an arrow out of the quiver, notching it on the string, controlling your breathing, and letting the arrow release itself. If you've per-

Philosophy class. Marin Headlands, San Francisco.
Courtesy of Patagonia

fected all the elements, you can't help but hit the center of the target. The same philosophy is true for climbing mountains. If you focus on the *process* of climbing, you'll end up on the summit. As it turns out, the perfect place I've found to apply this Zen philosophy is the business world.

Even as I taught our employees the Patagonia philosophy classes, I did not yet know what we would do to get our company out of the mess it was in. But I did know that we had become unsustainable and that we had to look to the Iroquois and their seven-generation planning, and not to corporate America, as models of stewardship and sustainability. As part of their decision process, the Iroquois had a person who represented the seventh generation in the future. If Patagonia could survive this crisis, we had to begin to make all our decisions as though we would be in business for a hundred years. We would grow only at a rate we could sustain for that long.

Teaching the classes also gave me my real answer to Dr. Kami's question. I knew, after thirty-five years, why I was in business. True, I wanted to give money to environmental causes. But even more, I wanted to create in Patagonia a model other businesses could look to in their own searches for environmental steward-ship and sustainability, just as our pitons and ice axes were models for other equip-ment manufacturers. Teaching the classes, I remembered again how I had become a businessman in the first place, that I had come home from the mountains with ideas spinning in my head on how to improve each piece of clothing and equip-ment I used. Teaching the classes, I realized how much Patagonia as a business was driven by its high quality standards and classic design principles. The products we made, each feature of every shirt, jacket, or pair of pants, had to be necessary.

Turnaround, in 1991, was fairly swift. Overnight we became a much more focused and sober-minded company, which limited its growth to a sustainable rate, spent carefully, and managed thoughtfully. Within three years we eliminated several layers of management, consolidated inventories into a single system, and brought the sales channels under central control. Having the philosophies in writing—as well as the shared cultural experience of the classes—played a critical role in the turnaround. I've heard that smart investors and bankers don't trust a growing company until it has proved itself by how it survives its first big crisis. If that's true, then we've been there.

I'm glad I didn't follow Dr. Kami's advice. If I had sold the company then and invested the proceeds in the stock market, I might not have much left to give to conservation causes now. If I hadn't stayed in business, I never would have realized—the hard way—the parallel between Patagonia's unsustainable push for growth and that of our whole industrial economy.

In 1992, *Inc.* magazine published a very negative article on Patagonia. The arti-cle concluded by questioning our chances of surviving the nineties: "Yvon Chouinard touts his company as a model for the future, when, in fact, its time may already have passed."

Well, we did survive through the millennium and in fact have been doing quite well. With a controlled growth rate of about 5 percent a year we have not only profited from our work but also received many awards for our business priorities. We were listed in *Working Mother* magazine as one of the "100 Best Companies for Working Mothers" and in *Fortune* magazine's "100 Best Companies to Work For." Our catalog and Web site have received twenty gold or silver awards from *Catalog Age* magazine. In 2004, Patagonia ranked fourteenth in the "Top 25 Medium Sized Businesses" by the Great Place to Work® Institute and the Society for Human Resource Management.

In 1994 we produced our first internal environmental assessment report, and from a life-cycle analysis commissioned on the four fibers we used the most—cotton, wool, polyester, and nylon—we learned that the most damaging for the environment was industrially grown cotton. By spring of

Kim Bennet training for breath holding. Waiamea Bay, Hawaii. *Crystal Thornburg*

1996 all Patagonia cotton clothing was switched over to 100 percent organically grown. In 1997 we created a line of organically grown cotton T-shirt blanks called Beneficial T's. In 1993 we were the first to start making our Synchilla jackets using fiber made from recycled polyester soda pop bottles.

Also in 1997 we started Water Girl USA, Inc. to make surfing- and water-inspired clothing for women. We also started the Rhythm line of rock-climbing clothes. These two labels along with Capilene are proving to be the fastest-growing parts of the company.

In 2004 we began work on what we call the Ocean Initiative. We envision the future of Patagonia to be a balance between mountain/wilderness activities and water/ocean–related products and sports.

As of 2004 we have about twenty company-owned stores in the United States and another fifteen in Europe and Japan. Most of these stores are old freestanding buildings that were saved from the wrecking ball. We built a warehouse in Reno, Nevada, that is state of the art in energy efficiency, and a three-story office building in Ventura was built using 95 percent recycled materials.

But more than any sales figure or even any product line, we are most proud of having given away twenty-two million dollars in cash and in-kind donations since 1985 to mostly grassroots conservational activists. We measure our success on the number of threats averted: old-growth forests that were not clear-cut, mines that were never dug in pristine areas, toxic pesticides that were not sprayed. We look to the tangible results of our support: the damaging dams dismantled, the rivers restored and listed as wild and scenic, the parks and wilderness areas created. We can't claim sole credit for these victories; we were merely funding the frontline activists. Patagonia either provided the seed money or was a major funder for many of these initiatives and victories.

The history of Patagonia from the crisis of 1991–92 to the present day doesn't make for such interesting reading, fortunately. By "interesting" I'm referring to the Chinese curse "May you live in interesting times." For the most part the big problems have been solved, and there were no crises except those that were invented by management to keep the company in yarak, a falconry term meaning when your falcon is superalert, hungry, but not weak, and ready to hunt. The story is really about how we are trying to live up to our mission statement: "Make the best product, cause no unnecessary harm, and use business to inspire and implement solutions to the environmental crisis."

Edwards Dam, before removal. In 1989 four environmental groups formed the Kennebec Coalition to convince the Federal Energy Regulatory Commission to remove the Edwards Dam and restore sea-run fish to the river. We at Patagonia helped by contributing money and creating and taking out public information ads in national and local papers. The dam came down in 2000, and already alewives, striped bass, shad, sturgeon, and salmon have moved into the seventeen miles of the longest stretch of spawning ground north of the Hudson. Next: Matilija, Lower Granite, Ice Harbor, Lower Monumental, Little Goose, Veazie, Great Works, etc. . . . *Scott Perry*

PHILOSOPHIES

PHILOSOPHIES

The philosophies are an expression of our values as they apply to different parts of the company. Our philosophies for design, production, distribution, image, human resources, finance, management, and the environment are each written specifically to guide Patagonia through the process of designing, manufacturing, and selling clothing. But they can be applied to any other kind of business as well. For instance, we use our design guidelines for making clothing as the basis of our philosophy of architecture and building.

What good does having a fixed set of written philosophies accomplish when everything else in the business world is so dynamic? How does Patagonia follow its philosophies in light of the expanding Internet market, the effects of NAFTA and GATT, dozens of technological leaps that significantly affect design and production, new and different employee demographics, and the ever-changing styles and lifestyles of customers?

The answer is that our philosophies aren't rules; they're guidelines. They're the keystones of our approach to any project, and although they are "set in stone," their application to a situation isn't. In every long-lasting business, the methods of conducting business may constantly change, but the values, the culture, and the philosophies remain constant.

At Patagonia, these philosophies must be communicated to everyone working in every part of the company, so that each of us becomes empowered with the knowledge of the right course to take, without having to follow a rigid plan or wait for orders from a "boss."

Living the values and knowing the philosophy of each part of the company align us all in a common direction, promote efficiency, and avoid the chaos that comes from poor communication.

We have made many mistakes during the past decade, but at no point have we lost our way for very long. We have the philosophies for a rough map, the only kind that's useful in a business world whose contours, unlike those of the mountains, change constantly and without much warning.

Holding piton. *Courtesy of Patagonia*

PRODUCT DESIGN PHILOSOPHY

Make the best product, cause no
unnecessary harm. . . .

The first part of our mission statement, "Make the best product," is the raison d'être of Patagonia and the cornerstone of our business philosophy. Striving to make the best *quality* product is the reason we got into business in the first place. We are a product-driven company, and without a tangible product there would obviously be no business and the other goals of our mission statement would thus be irrelevant. Having quality, useful products anchors our business in the real world and allows us to expand our mission.

QUALITY AND SURFBOARDS

When my son, Fletcher, was a teenager, I told him it didn't matter to me what he wanted to do for work in the future as long as he also learned some sort of craft that involved working with his hands. He chose shaping surfboards, which was a good fit since he is slightly dyslexic, and dyslexics often have a great sense of proportion. They make good sculptors.

A few years later, after he had decided to devote his life's work to making surfboards, I tried to encourage him to make better surfboards. "I can't do that," he said. "I can't make a better board than Al or Rusty. They make the best boards. They perform the best."

I said, "But if pro surfers go on a trip to Tahiti or Indonesia, they have to take six to ten boards because they're going to break at least half of them. You call that good quality?"

"But everyone's boards break like that," he answered.

We realized that durability was not among the primary criteria for the overall quality of surfboards. In fact surfboards were just a fashion item, because naive young victims often insist on buying the same style boards as the world champion. You can imagine how well that works for them!

Once I persuaded Fletcher to make a better surfboard, he had to identify all the criteria that define quality and performance as they pertain to surfboards.

For quality, he would first have to include all the elements that make up the aesthetics of the finish: no "sand-through" on the glassing, no air bubbles, sharp pin stripes, etc. Then he would have to look at the traits affecting the board's durability, such as breaking strength, compression strength (heel pressure dings), resistance to ultraviolet degradation, strength of the fin boxes, water absorption by the foam, etc. Performance has a few major elements such as hull speed, turnability, and paddling characteristics. There are also some criteria more difficult to define, like "responsiveness" and timbre and flex.

Next Fletcher had to research all kinds of different foams, various kinds of wood and other materials for the board's stringers, fiberglass cloths, and resins for the exterior. Hundreds of panels were made and tested for strength, lightness, flex, resistance to delamination. At the same time, he had to shape thousands of boards until he was confident that it wouldn't be his shaping skill that held him back.

The end result is that his boards are lighter, stronger, perform as well as, and last much longer than other surfboards. Even though the average surfer still doesn't understand or demand quality in his or her surfboards, Fletcher does.

—Y. C.

Because we had a history of making the best climbing tools in the world, tools that your life is dependent on, we couldn't be satisfied making second-best clothing. Our clothes—from Baggies to flannel shirts, from underwear to outerwear—have to be the best of their kind. Trying to make the best product also inspires us to create the best child care center and the best production department and to be the best at our jobs.

"Make the best" is a difficult goal. It doesn't mean "among the best" or the "best at a particular price point." It means "make the best," period.

What makes a product the best of its kind? Early in our history our chief designer for many years, Kate Larramendy, issued me a challenge. She said that we didn't make the best clothing in the world, and moreover, if we did, we'd go out of business.

"Why?" I asked her.

"Because the best shirt in the world is Italian," she said. "It's made from handwoven fabric, with hand-sewn buttons and buttonholes, and impeccably finished. And it costs three hundred dollars. Our customers wouldn't pay that."

Surfboard shaper Fletcher Chouinard.
Amy Kumler

I asked, "What would happen if you threw that three-hundred-dollar shirt into your washer and dryer?"

"Oh, you'd never do that. It would shrink. It has to be dry-cleaned."

To me a shirt that has to be treated so delicately has diminished value. Because I think ease of care is an important attribute, I would never own a shirt like that, much less make and sell one.

If my design chief and I could view quality so differently, then clearly we had to hash out what criteria we should consider for Patagonia. Webster's defines *quality* as "a degree of excellence," and of course the best quality would be the highest degree. Some people believe that quality is subjective, that excellence for one person may be mediocrity for another. But then they may be thinking of *taste*, which means "individual preference." My design chief and I finally had to agree that quality *is* absolutely objective and definable; otherwise we would never even be able to establish our design criteria.

We ended up with a checklist of criteria for Patagonia's designers to consider, and the list applies equally to other businesses. With clearly defined quality criteria for all aspects of a product, it becomes a straightforward matter to judge which are the best clothes—or automobiles, wines, or hamburgers. Here are the main questions a Patagonia designer must ask about each product to see if it fits our standards.

Is It Functional?

It may be that someday fashion historians will credit Patagonia for inspiring men to go beyond gray sweatshirts and wear colorful clothes in the outdoors, but what I hope they remember is that we were one of the first to apply industrial design principles to clothing design.

The first precept of industrial design is that the function of an object should determine its design and materials. Every design at Patagonia begins with a functional need. A piece of thermal underwear must wick and breathe and dry quickly. A paddling jacket has not only to repel and seal out water but also to allow a full range of arm movement. Function must dictate form.

In the fashion business, design often begins with the fabric, and then a use is thought up for it. At Patagonia, the fabric is often the last item to be chosen, although a new fabric can also spark innovation for products, as when I stumbled on those polyester football jerseys and saw the potential for underwear. The superficial aspects of a fabric are not important; rather, we're interested in the substance.

Even with sportswear, we start with functional considerations. Is this shirt needed for hot, tropical or hot, dry weather? What kind of drape or fit does it require? Does it need to be loosely woven to dry quickly or densely enough to blunt a mosquito's sharp proboscis? Only after we determine a product's functional need do we begin researching fabrics. From the other end, our fabric department is always working to create fabrics from materials that cause less harm, such as hemp, bamboo, and recycled polyester, and then we incorporate them into the line.

Designing from the foundation of filling a functional need focuses the design process and ultimately makes for a superior finished product. Without a serious functional demand we can end up with a product that, although it may look great, is difficult to rationalize as being in our line—i.e., "Who needs it?"

Is It Multifunctional?

Why buy two pieces of gear when one will do the work of both? Making products as versatile as possible derives from our origins as mountain climbers who had to haul our gear up the mountain on our backs, not in the trunk of an SUV.

Besides, to carry as little as possible in the mountains is a spiritual tenet of many outdoor enthusiasts, as well as a practical consideration. John Muir liked to limit his "supplies" to a tin cup, a loaf of stale bread, and an overcoat. Now it's an environmental consideration as well. Everything we personally own that's made, sold, shipped, stored, cleaned, and ultimately thrown away does some environmental harm every step of the way, harm that we're either directly responsible for or is done on our behalf.

All the more reason, when we consider the purchase of anything, to ask ourselves, both as producers and consumers: Is this purchase necessary? Do I really need a new outfit to do yoga? Can I do well enough with something I already have? And will it do more than one thing?

We used to make a small rock-climbing pack that had a thin foam pad in the back for comfort. The pad was removable so you could take it out and sit on it on cold bivouacs. My climbing partner broke his arm in a fall in the Tetons, and I was able to make a perfect splint with the sheet of foam and a few accessory straps.

The more you know, the less you need. The experienced fly fisherman with only one rod, one type of fly, and one type of line will always outfish the duffer with an entire quiver of gear and flies. I never forget Thoreau's advice: "I say beware of all enterprises that require new clothes. . . ."

Sometimes a product designed for one activity turns out to work surprisingly well for another. A substantial percentage of the climbing jackets we make end up on the ski slopes rather than granite walls, even though we tailor our marketing efforts to climbers. We try to keep anomalies like that in mind. The best products are multifunctional, however you market them. If the climbing jacket you bought to ski in can also be worn over your suit during a snowstorm in Paris or New York, we've saved you from having to buy two jackets, one of which would stay in the closet nine months of the year. Buy less; buy better. Make fewer styles; design better.

Still, we also make some narrow-use, sport-specific products for climbing and skiing (jackets), fly-fishing (vests, jackets, waders, boots), surfing (shorts), and paddling (Lotus Designs jackets, dry tops, life vests). We do so for two reasons. First, for the sports we serve, we want to outfit our customers from cap to socks, and this is part of our bond with the customer. The second reason is credibility. To be respected as an outfitter to skiers or fly fishers we make the critical products that show we know what we're doing—the best ski jackets, the best fishing vests.

Is It Durable?

This question also derives from our origins in climbing gear, which has to stand up to hard, prolonged use, and has become a factor in our environmental philosophy as well. Because the overall durability of a product is only as good as its weakest element, the ultimate goal should be a product whose parts wear out at

Some of my favorite tools are axes made by Gränsfors Bruks AB of Sweden, which has been manufacturing axes since 1902. *This essay came from the front of its catalog.*

RESPONSIBILITY FOR THE TOTAL

What we take, how and what we make, what we waste, is in fact a question of ethics. We have unlimited responsibility for the Total. A responsibility which we try to take, but do not always succeed in. One part of this responsibility is the quality of the products and how many years the product will maintain its durability.

To make a high quality product is a way to pay respect and responsibility to the customer and the user of the product. A high quality product, in the hands of those who have learned how to use it and how to look after it, will very likely be more durable. This is good for the owner, the user. But this is good as well as part of a greater whole: increased durability means that we take less (decreased consumption of material and energy), that we need to produce less (gives us more time to do other things we think are important or enjoyable), destroy less (less waste).

—Gränsfors Bruks AB
S-820 70 Bergsjö, Sweden
Phone: +46 652 71090,
Fax: +46 652 14002
Email: axes@gransfors.com

roughly the same time and only after a long life. You may notice that a great product like Levi's jeans will get a hole in the knee at about the same time you notice a hole in the rear or in the pocket. Conversely, the worst examples for wear range from electronics equipment, which have become virtually disposable when one element fails, to a pair of pricey swim shorts whose elastic waistband loses its stretch from the chlorine in pools while the rest of the garment still looks new.

Some of our customers will not give up on their Patagonia clothes until it becomes a matter of indecency, like a favorite pair of jeans. *Kathy Metcalf*

Technically, those shorts, as well as the electronics equipment, can be repaired, but because the cost of repair is too high relative to the original purchase price, the product usually gets junked.

Someone once said that the poor can't afford to buy cheap goods. You can buy a cheap blender that will burn out the first time you try to grind some ice cubes, or you can wait until you can afford a quality one that will last. Ironically, the longer you wait, the less you may have to spend; at my age, it's becoming easier to buy only products that will "last a lifetime."

To get all the components of a Patagonia product to be roughly equal in durability, we test continually in both the lab and the field. We test until something fails, strengthen that part, then see what fails next, strengthen that, etc., until we're confident that the product is durable as a whole. There's always going to be a need for repairs, and we make sure that they're possible; a zipper should be replaceable without the entire coat having to be taken apart.

Does It Fit Our Customer?

People who aren't in the clothing business can count themselves lucky not to have the problem of fit. The way a company sizes clothes—what you call a small or a medium, whether you design for physically fit people or those who aren't—will always satisfy some customers and distress and turn away others. At Patagonia we pattern our sizes to our core customers, who are active and in better shape than the average snowmobiler or bait fisherman. This may mean we lose potential customers in order to keep our core customers happier. So be it.

Fit should also be consistent throughout the line. Someone who wears a medium in one style shirt should expect to wear a medium in another style. Any piece of clothing should fit right off the shelf without washing, and it should not shrink over its lifetime.

Functional clothing poses other questions of fit that have to be carefully thought through. Will the product be worn over other layers or against the skin? A product designed with a close fit for climbing may also be worn by snowboarders or skiers who want a looser fit. In that case, the climber, as the core customer for that product, wins (the snowboarder or casual use customer can size up if she or he wants to).

Is It as Simple as Possible?

Simplify, simplify.

—H. D. THOREAU

One "simplify" would have sufficed.

—RALPH WALDO EMERSON, IN RESPONSE

Koshun Miyamoto once complimented his fencing teacher's wife on the beauty of her gravel garden, a square of coarse-grained sand, set off by three stones from a nearby stream that conveyed a "powerful, evocative image of space and balance." The fencing teacher's wife protested that the garden wasn't complete and wouldn't be until she could "express the same feeling it has now using only one stone instead of three."

The functionally driven design is usually minimalist. Or as Dieter Rams, head of design at Braun, maintains, "Good design is as little design as possible."

Complexity is often a sure sign that the functional needs have not been solved. Take the difference between the Ferrari and the Cadillac of the 1960s. The Ferrari's clean lines suited its high-performance aims. The Cadillac really didn't have functional aims. It didn't have the steering, suspension, torque, aerodynamics, or brakes appropriate to its immense horsepower. But then nothing about its design really had to work. All it had to do was convey the idea of power, creature comfort, of a living room floating down the highway to the golf course. So, to a basically ugly shape were added all manner of useless chrome gingerbread: fins at the back, breasts at the front. Once you lose the discipline of functionality as a design guidepost, the imagination goes amok. Once you design a monster, it tends to look like one too.

A great mountain jacket does not look like a 1960s Cadillac decked out in fabric. Stronger, lighter fabrics eliminate the need for ballistics cloth reinforcements at the shoulders and elbows. Newer, more breathable fabrics let us do away with the heavy, awkward pit zips once necessary for ventilation. Make the front zipper sufficiently watertight, and you can dispense with the weight and bulk of a protective wind flap.

Is the Product Line Simple?

Some choices are simple: Do you want your goat cheese plain or with chives? But most choices for consumers aren't that simple. Few of us have the time, patience, or knowledge to order from a twelve-page Chinese restaurant menu or to choose among a hundred pairs of seemingly identical skis in a ski shop.

People have too many choices these days. They are tired of constantly having to make decisions, particularly when it takes a major effort to make *intelligent* decisions—i.e., knowing the difference between all the breathable/waterproof fabrics. For most people, separating the men's styles from the women's is hard enough. The best restaurants in the world have set menus, and the best ski shops have already decided which skis are best for your skill level.

Since function comes first at Patagonia, we avoid the smorgasbord approach. We don't systematically rip off our competitors' most popular styles to end up with twenty functionally identical ski pants. Nevertheless, from time to time our own line gets too big; the differences between products become too small. When that happens, we know that Patagonia is not living up to its own philosophy.

When we're doing our job right, each style of ski pant has a distinct purpose. We make each in a good range of sizes (including women's) and offer just enough colors. Then we work in long-term partnership with a contractor to produce those pants as efficiently as possible year after year. Along the way we make periodic, mostly incremental improvements that render the product simpler and lighter, more durable, more breathable, more agile. Our constancy tells the customers that we believe in our products, that they are the best we know how to make.

When we deviate from our philosophy, for whatever reason, we pay a steep price. In the fall of 1991 we offered men and women's flannel shirts in twenty-five different patterns and colors. The idea was to make them in equal but limited quantities and let the customers decide which ones they preferred. The best sellers we would quickly reorder, and the "dogs" we would put on sale. But we neglected to take into account the cost of having to design, produce, warehouse, and catalog a product that required 125 stock-keeping units. We had no equation showing us the exponentially greater amount of time each pattern would add to our work.

If a proliferation of colors and patterns drains profit, think what a mushrooming of styles can do. We've worked out an interesting formula. Each product Patagonia adds to the line (without dropping an old one) requires the hiring of two and one-half new people.

The best-performing firms make a narrow range of products very well. The best firms' products also use up to 50 percent fewer parts than those made by their less successful rivals. Fewer parts mean a faster, simpler (and usually cheaper) manufacturing process. Fewer parts mean less to go wrong; quality comes built in. And although the best companies need fewer workers to look after quality control, they also have fewer defects and generate less waste.

In business heaven we shall all have businesses making simple products like WD-40, or bottled water that we could sell for two to four times as much as gasoline.

Is It an Innovation or an Invention?

There are two types of creativity: the creativity of making
zero to one, and the creativity of making one to 1,000.
—Kazuhiko Nishi, the "Steve Jobs of Japan"

When I die and go to hell, the devil is going to make me the marketing director for a cola company. I'll be in charge of trying to sell a product that no one
needs, is identical to its competition, and can't be sold on its merits. I'd be competing head-on in the cola wars, on price, distribution, advertising, and promotion,
which would indeed be hell for me. Remember, I'm the kid who couldn't play
competitive games. I'd much rather design and sell products so good and unique
that they have no competition.

Successful inventing requires a tremendous amount of energy, time, and money.
The big inventions are so rare that even the most brilliant geniuses think up only a
few marketable inventions in their lifetimes. It may take thirty years to come up

Surfing the Ventura
Overhead, c. 1998. In
the early seventies my
surfboard shaper Greg
Liddle and I designed
this surf kayak. We started
with the premise that we
were surfers who wanted
to ride a wave on a kayak
as opposed to being
kayakers who wanted
to surf. Approaching the
design from a surfer's
perspective resulted in
a unique eight-foot-long
"surf/yak" with three fins
and a closed kayak deck
on top. *Rick Ridgeway*

The RURP, or realized ultimate reality piton, was one of our few real inventions. It was made of tough chrome-nickel steel and is used to chisel its way into incipient cracks. *Courtesy of Patagonia*

with an invention, but within a few years or months there can be a thousand innovations spawned from that original idea. Innovation can be achieved much more quickly because you already start with an existing product idea or design.

Some companies are based on having proprietary designs and patents, but far more successful ones are based on innovation. Just compare the success of the classic inventor country, the United States, with the ultimate innovator, Japan Inc. In the clothing fashion business especially, there is simply no time for long, drawn-out pure research. Patagonia didn't invent bunting fleece. The idea came from my seeing Doug Tompkins wearing a brushed wool Fila pullover. Since it could only be dry-cleaned, it was impractical for outdoor use, but it spawned an idea that led to polyester bunting, Synchilla, and a host of microfleeces.

We adapted the design for Stand Up Shorts from a pair of double-seated English corduroy shorts, and the idea for our very successful Baggies came from a pair of nylon shorts I spotted in an Oxnard department store. The ultimate Patagonia versions are more functional, durable, and far superior to the knocked-off originals, especially for their intended active outdoor use. Like creative cooks, we view "originals" as recipes for inspiration, and then we close the book to do our own thing. The inspirations for some of our best designs are like the fusion recipes of the best chefs.

Is It a Global Design?

You'll never know if you're making the best products in the world until they're sold and used all over the globe. But this creates challenges of its own.

Imagine two companies, Tomatoes-R-Us and Acme Tomatoes. Both sell tomatoes worldwide. Tomatoes-R-Us grows all its tomatoes on huge agribusiness farms in California's San Joaquin Valley. Its product is square and firm, travels well, and can be easily ripened with ethylene gas after it reaches a foreign port and before it reaches the consumer. It can compete, sharply, on price worldwide because it has state-of-the-art machines, hybrid seeds, chemicals, and cost accountants, plus heavily subsidized public water and export subsidies.

In contrast, Acme prefers to grow its tomatoes in the country in which they are sold: plum tomatoes for the Italian pasta market and juicy, vine-ripened tomatoes to the picky French.

To me, Tomatoes-R-Us is merely a U.S. company doing international business. Acme, on the other hand, is a global company because it knows the importance of tailoring its products to specific markets.

Patagonia is a California company. Our corporate culture, lifestyle, and design sense are still purely California. This helps us in some ways, because California is so polyglot and racially and culturally diverse. Where else could you find a Szechwan enchilada? But I would not yet define Patagonia as a global company until we learn to think, design, and produce beyond our present limits. When we become a global company, not just a business operating internationally, we'll adapt our designs toward local preferences, toward their functional need and sizing and color. We'll produce more locally and less centrally. Most important, thinking and acting more globally will open our minds to an endless possibility of new ideas, some of which we can adapt to use in our domestic market.

The hottest place right now for surf fashion is Australia. For years I've been going to Japan for inspiration about all sorts of things. The Japanese import only the best of Western culture. The best blues music, Italian fashion design, and French wine all can be found in Tokyo.

Is It Easy to Care For and Clean?

When we studied the environmental impacts of clothing throughout its life cycle (i.e., fabric manufacture, dyeing, construction, distribution, care by the consumer, and disposal), we were surprised to find that two of the biggest villains were transportation and cleaning. In particular, we found that the postsale care of a clothing product caused as much as four times the amount of harm as the entire manufacturing process.

Also, maintenance of any product is a chore, and for that reason alone, low maintenance becomes a criterion for high quality. At Patagonia none of us likes to iron or bother with the dry cleaners, and we assume that our customers don't either. We have practical reasons too. You should be able to wash travel clothes in a sink or in a cooking pot, then hang them out to dry in a hut and still look decent for the plane ride home.

But environmental concerns trump all others. Ironing is an inefficient use of electricity, washing in hot water wastes energy, and dry cleaning uses toxic chemicals. Machine drying, far more than actual wear, shortens the life of a garment—just check the lint filter!

The most responsible way for a consumer and a good citizen to buy clothes is to buy used clothing. Beyond that, avoid buying clothes you have to dry-clean or iron. Wash in cold water. Line dry when possible. Wear your shirt more than one day before you wash it. Consider faster-drying alternatives to 100 percent cotton for your travel clothes.

Does It Have Any Added Value?

A study by Dr. Thomas M. Power at the University of Montana states that only 10 to 15 percent of the money Americans spend on goods and services is necessary for survival. You don't need to eat filet mignon to be healthy, you don't need to live in a four-thousand-square-foot house to be sheltered, and you don't need a pair of fifty-dollar surf trunks in order to go in the water. People spend the other 85 percent to 90 percent of their money for upgrades in quality. They'll pay extra for the added value of a pound of filet mignon over a pound of hamburger, even though either one would meet their nutritional needs.

Unlike those who made claims in the cola wars, we do add real value. We make durable, high-quality goods that function well outdoors. We design everything we make to be the best of its kind, and whatever doesn't measure up goes back to the drawing board. Moreover, we carefully define, rather than just assert, what makes each product the best of its kind. Durability and low environmental impact make that list. Fleeting fashion and the illusion of luxury do not.

We treat customers with respect too. Customer phone service as a rule has become so terrible in this country—thanks to transaction quotas, intentionally long hold times, and managerial indifference—that it would be easy to shine without much effort, if only because we don't farm out phone calls to a service bureau in Delhi. But we make the extra step anyway.

We have an "ironclad" guarantee, and we honor it—even if we have to go to great lengths. As an example, a customer once returned a well-used, very old pair of pants, hoping they could be repaired. They were well beyond repair, and we made the mistake of discarding them. The customer was not happy; she wanted her favorite pair of pants back, whatever shape they were in. We offered her a replacement pair (in a newer, improved style), no charge, but she wanted the same style, and color, as the pair she had sent us. Fair enough. We went to the archives, found the pattern, then managed to find a bolt of the right fabric in the right color. Before long the customer had her old-style pants back, now brand-new.

IRONCLAD GUARANTEE

We guarantee everything we make. If you are not satisfied with one of our products at the time you receive it, or if one of our products does not perform to your satisfaction, return it to the store you bought it from or to Patagonia for repair, replacement or refund. Damage due to wear and tear will be repaired at a reasonable charge.

WE GUARANTEE EVERYTHING WE MAKE

After climbing Denali, Rick Ridgeway and I celebrated by going down to Homer, Alaska, "a quaint little drinking village with a fishing problem," to dig for razor clams. After this photo appeared in our catalog, we received a letter from Robert Mondavi, who had identified that we had been drinking his wine. Rather than send a cease-and-desist letter, he thanked us and invited us up to a VIP tour of the winery. *Peter Hackett*

Not every customer service transaction is so involved or costly, but we do know that the extra steps we take are worth the trouble. Our catalog reorder rate from customers, season after season, far exceeds the mail-order industry standard. In fact it's off the charts.

As in the case of the pants that couldn't be allowed to die, the value of our products sometimes seems to grow over time. In Tokyo there are stores that deal only in vintage Patagonia clothing.

In 1998, I was at the opening celebration of our store in Shibuya, Tokyo, with two or three hundred of our best customers enjoying the drinks and sushi.

Suddenly the room went quiet except for the sucking-through-the-teeth sound the Japanese make to indicate shock or pleasure. A young fellow had made a grand entrance wearing an old Patagonia jacket. Everyone in the room knew that the jacket was a 1979 Borglite pile and that he had paid a fortune for it.

The Patagonia label is evocative and valued in the marketplace. But we don't use it as a crutch for mediocre design. A product independent of the label should stand on its own merits and not rely on the label to "carry" it. The product must be intrinsically valuable in its own right. A Patagonia product should be identifiable even from a distance by the quality of workmanship and attention to detail. The Zen master would say a true Patagonia product doesn't need any label.

Is It Authentic?

I once saw someone wearing a sweatshirt that said "authentic" on the chest, and nothing else. The fashion industry is so caught up with this idea of "authentic" that it has become another of those meaningless words. However, our customers expect us to make the real thing. Just as a field coat has to have a bloodproof, lined game pocket in the back, and work pants have to be made for real carpenters, roofers, and masons, if we offer a rugby shirt, it has to be made to play rugby in.

We made a mistake in 1975, when we contracted out our rugby shirts to a fashion manufacturer in Hong Kong. We again made a mistake with rugby shirts in 2002. This time we brought back our rugby shirts, authentic in every way—rubber buttons, heavy, tough knit fabric, reinforced stitching everywhere—except we made them in fashionable color stripes; they didn't sell. They were not authentic rugby colors. We finally got it right in 2005.

Is It Art?

Solving a serious functional need is not always required in our clothing designs, particularly in our sportswear. We don't always have to bow first to the god of pure function. Patagonia clothes should also be fun, and they can be art. Fashion is happening only now, and art is timeless. In fact fashion is always passé because it is a response to an event in the past. It may recycle someday, but it will certainly be dead tomorrow.

When I think about clothing as art, I imagine a Navajo Indian blanket coat worn by an eighty-year-old woman. Her silver hair is tied back in a bun. She could be rich; she could be poor. She could have bought the coat in 1940, or it could have once belonged to her mother. The coat is authentic and a classic, not a modern version of a traditional blanket coat. It's a work of art. She could give the coat to her granddaughter, who could wear it for another fifty years, and it would still be in style. It is priceless.

The difference between fashion and art is the difference between a 1950s Hawaiian shirt you can buy in a thrift shop for a dollar and one you have to pay three thousand dollars for in a vintage aloha shirt store. The former has bright colors and a "Hawaiian" design, while the latter has the aesthetic quality of a matched pocket and collar, the artistic qualities of the print, and the drape and feel of good fabric. One is junk, and one is art. It's the difference between illustration and art in painting. An illustrator becomes an artist when he or she can convey the same emotion with fewer brushstrokes.

ZEN

Cold air from the valley drifts upward. It's predawn, and I've been moving on the Nose of El Cap through the night, focused on the rock in front of me in the faint light of my headlamp. Suddenly, I think of how tired and exposed I am, alone, rope-less, far past any point of retreat. A surge of panic courses through me. I try to think of the summit, but that thought too is dangerous.

An image floats into my mind. I'm following my father in the early morning through a pasture in the White Mountains in New Hampshire. He strides toward Moosebrook, his favorite fishing spot. I'm not even half his height, and the frosty grass brushes all the way up to my waist.

We reach the river. My dad skips from rock to rock, downstream to the first hole, and looks back for me. The water is freezing, and the rocks are covered in slime. I'm afraid to follow. I burrow painfully through the thickets of pricker bushes, swamp, and blackflies as my father calls for me. The bugs chase me back to the river's edge, and I timidly wade in and try to catch up. Tense and anxious, I lose my footing and fall into the river. I gasp for breath in the icy water but manage to scramble onto a rock, where I bawl until my father comes back. "I don't like fishing. I want to go home."

My father shakes his head at me, and his eyes sparkle. "Dean, put everything aside. There's nothing to be afraid of, except a little cold water. Just focus on the next step you are taking. I feel so happy running down the river, sun reflecting off the water, my body naturally going where it's supposed to. I almost don't think at all. I just respond to what's in front of me."

He stops talking and heads downstream again. We slowly pick our way across the rocks, catching rainbows and brook trout. The day passes quickly, and my confidence rises. Soon I'm playing and racing down the rapids with eyes wide and senses alert, not knowing I've just received my first lesson in Zen.

The air drifts over my body. I grasp the immediate. I reach for the next hold.

—Dean Potter

Dean Potter, free soloing astroman on the Washington Column, Yosemite. *Eric Perlman*

Are We Just Chasing Fashion?

Because of our commitment to quality, we run at such a slow pace that we're the turtles in the fashion race. Our design and product development calendar is usually eighteen months long, too long even to be a contender in any new fads. We rarely buy off-the-shelf fabrics, and we don't buy existing prints, so we have to work with artists and design studios in producing original art. With our organic cotton products, we often have to begin the design and manufacturing process with bales of raw cotton. Then we have to conduct tests all through the process, from the fabric lab to the field. We need time to do our "homework," showing the potential product to core customers, buyers, retail store employees, to see if it will sell or if we should even make it. Every time we try to chase fashion we end up being six months or a year too late—and we look stupid.

Are We Designing for Our Core Customer?

All our customers are not equal in our eyes. There are indeed some we favor more than others. These are our core customers, those for whom we actually design our clothes. To understand this more clearly, we can look at our customers as if they existed in a series of concentric circles. In the center, or core circle, are our intended customers. These people are the dirt-baggers who, in most cases, have trouble even affording our clothes. A couple of specific examples will help.

Audrey Sutherland is an amazing Hawaiian grandmother. Her life revolves around long inflatable kayak trips—solo. She's logged more than eight thousand miles along the coasts of Alaska and British Columbia, seventy-seven hundred of which were solo, and thousands more miles in the Greek isles, Scotland, and Hawaii. About paddling these trips alone she says, "You become so much more part of the natural world around you; you're communicating as if you were a rock or bush or a fish. You become part of the elements." Audrey's other advice: "Don't spend money on gear. Spend it on airplane tickets." Even in her eighties she continues to do serious trips in the North Pacific.

When Dean Potter climbs the Nose of El Capitan in Yosemite, he doesn't need to take along any rain gear because he's back in camp for lunch. As one of our product testers, though, he gives us great feedback on the gear he does use. People like Dean and our other climbing, surfing, kayaking ambassadors and the hundreds of professionals on our Pro Purchase Program, which provides our product at a preferred rate to exceptional athletes and working outdoor professionals, are among the best in the world at what they do. They are the innovators, and their actions define the state of the art in their fields.

Have We Done Our Homework?

Some people think we're a successful company because we're willing to take risks, but I'd say that's only partly true. What they don't realize is that we do our homework. A few years back when we switched midstream from polypropylene to Capilene for our underwear fabric, we had done our fabric development, we

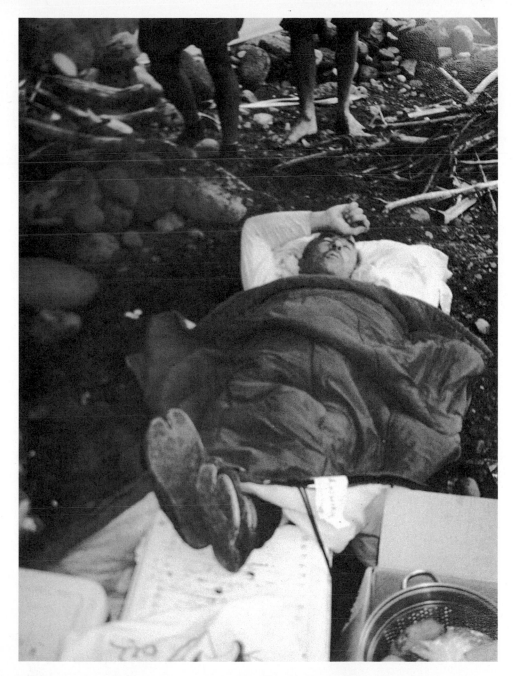

Reefwalkers are sold in fishing stores in Hawaii, where I first saw them. I thought they would make a great shoe for all sorts of water sports. Strangely, no one else at work was very enthused about them. Kris McDivitt wrote with indelible ink on one of the roof beams of the office, "My boss made me order 20,000 pair of Reefwalkers," and had me sign it! Years later on a sea kayaking trip around the north side of Molokai in Hawaii, I fell while bouldering, broke my elbow in three pieces, and had to be rescued. I was wearing Reefwalkers at the time. *Rell Sunn*

Product testing in
"full" Scottish conditions.
C. 1969. *Doug Tompkins*

had done our testing in the fabric lab. We made tops and bottoms with half the garment Capilene and half polypropylene and extensively tested them in the field. We knew the market, and we were absolutely confident that it was the right thing to do.

Patagonia design routinely ventures into the unknown, where doing all your research still doesn't tell you yes or no and you have to make a decision. We took a chance on importing twenty thousand pairs of Reefwalkers from Japan—they were tabis with felt soles for walking on slippery rocks—and we had to eat them. On the other side, we took a chance on changing from polypro to Capilene, and it worked. Miss or hit, the Patagonia design environment encourages individualism. Personal risk, whether it's climbing a mountain, taking on debts to develop a dream, or designing a product that surprises is a valued part of the Patagonia culture in general and of the design environment in particular. Market trends are less important than strong intuition.

Although we encourage everyone at Patagonia to be "gonzo," to stick his or her neck out, we don't want to become martyrs. You can think of martyrs as being victims, or you can think of them as just being people too far ahead of their time. The problem with risk taking of course is that it's risky! Reefwalkers were not a financial success. Capilene was. You can minimize risk by doing your research and, most of all, by testing. Testing is an integral part of the Patagonia industrial design process, and it needs to be included in every part of this process. It involves testing competitors' products, "quick and dirty" testing of new ideas to see if they are worth pursuing, fabric testing, "living" with a new product to judge how "hot" the sales may be, testing production samples for function and durability, etc., and test marketing a product to see if people will buy it.

Is It Timely?

*If everyone thinks you have a good idea,
you're too late.*

— Paul Hawken

Business is a race to see who can be the first to bring a product to the customer, and inventions and ideas are often born simultaneously around the world by any number of unrelated individuals. It's almost as if every idea had its time.

In 1971 at Chouinard Equipment we introduced our Hexentric style of climbing chocks. This was a big expenditure for us in dies and tooling because the chocks came in ten sizes. After a few months on the market a friend of ours, Mike Sherrick, gave us an idea about how they could be redesigned to be more versatile. Within two weeks a climber in Norway wrote to us with the same idea. We immediately scrapped all our tooling, invested in all new dies, and in 1972 came out with the new "polycentric" Hexentrics. Ironically, that very same month a competitor came out with exact copies of our old, and now obsolete, style of hexentric chocks.

In 1980 the average life span of a hard goods product was three years. Now it is three months or less.

There is no time to do "hard" tooling anymore. You make a chip and put it on a computer-aided milling machine or lathe, and you can produce parts in hours instead of months or years. Being first offers tremendous marketing advantages, not the least of which is you have no competition. Coming in second, even with a superior product at a better price, is often no substitute for just plain being first. This doesn't mean we should be "chasing" trends or products. It applies more to "discovering" a new fabric or a new process. Again, the key word is *discovering* instead of *inventing*. There's simply no time for inventing.

Maintaining a sense of urgency throughout a company is one of the most difficult challenges in business. The problem is further compounded by having to depend on outside suppliers who may not have the same sense of expediency. I constantly hear people giving lame excuses for why something is impossible or why a job didn't get done on time. Here are a few examples:

"I wish I could help you but . . ." How many times have you heard service persons say those words when you know they don't mean it and are just being lazy? "I wish I could give you a baked potato instead of rice, but we have a no substitution policy here." Or, "I wish we could do it, but our insurance policy won't allow it." Why not just do it anyway? Or get another insurance policy or don't even have insurance? Get out of the kitchen if you can't stand the heat.

"We can't get any more fabric (or aluminum or whatever)." Substitute another material; try another mill or fifty or a hundred mills. Try mills in other countries; call a competitor and find out where it get its fabric.

"I've called and called, but I can't get through." How many times have you really called? Three or four times? Call twenty times. Or try a telegram or a registered letter, or catch him at home with a 5:00 A.M. wake-up call.

"The computer screwed up." At least people didn't have this one fifty years ago! Computers don't screw up; people screw up. Garbage in, garbage out. *"All the computer terminals are tied up."* This may be true, but maybe the job could have been done on a typewriter or with a yellow no. 2 Eberhard Faber.

"I didn't have the time" or *"I've been too busy"* to answer your letter, to return your call, to write a weekly report, to clean my desk, whatever. This is a dishonest excuse. What the person really means is that the job didn't get done because it had the lowest priority, and in fact he may never return your call because he really doesn't want to. People do what they want to do.

Lastly, *"Impossible."* The lamest of the lame excuses! Difficult maybe, or impractical, or too expensive, but rarely is anything impossible.

To stay ahead of the competition, our ideas have to come from as close to the source as possible. With technical products, our "source" is the dirtbag core customer. He's the one using the products and finding out what works, what doesn't, and what is needed.

On the contrary, sales representatives, shop owners, salesclerks, and people in focus groups are usually not visionaries. They can tell you only what is happening now: what is in fashion, what the competition is doing, and what is selling. They are a good source of information if you want to be a player in the "cola wars," but the information is too old if you want to have leading-edge products.

Does It Cause Any Unnecessary Harm?

The responsibility for the quality of our clothing begins with the designers. Similarly, the second part of our mission statement, "cause no unnecessary harm," is also largely the responsibility of the designers and production managers.

Our ongoing environmental assessment of our materials and our manufacturing processes gives us information about the true effects of our business. Sometimes that information leads us to ask more questions, and sometimes we are left with a tug-of-war between the "best quality" and "causing no harm." For instance, we took a quality hit in 1990, when we first used recycled paper in our catalog. But the next catalog was better, and now the recycled paper we use is perfectly adequate.

Of course, we will never make clothes out of any industrial-grown cotton again. We will try not to use toxic dyes, we will try to use recycled materials, and we will seek to do business only with other responsible companies. But we can never be satisfied with our progress. Growing cotton, even organically, is still not the best use for valuable farmland. Recycling some of our wastes and making Synchilla jackets out of recycled soda pop bottles are not enough.

We have to take responsibility for what we make, from birth to death and then

HOW TO SEED A DRESS

We have been driving for several hours up winding roads high into the mountains of China's Shaanxi Province. I am here to visit the fields where our hemp is grown. Hemp farming is complex and difficult to understand without seeing it firsthand.

At the end of this long, isolated road I expect to see no more than one field with a farmer. I am surprised to find an entire village in a flurry of activity. Most of the fields were harvested three weeks ago, but there is still a small one left standing, saved for my visit. This remote region of China is experiencing a drought, and the height of the crop is short this year. The hemp grown here is rain-fed. There is no irrigation, and no chemicals are used. This is the way it has always been done here. Fertilization comes compliments of the chickens and cattle that roam freely in the fields. These hemp farmers have no need for herbicides or insecticides.

Most of the villagers are busy getting the hemp ready to be delivered to the mill that weaves our fabric. Bundles of hemp stand in the field to dry. Seeds are being separated from the stalks, which are then carried to the river and submerged for retting (a process that loosens the fiber from the woody pulp). I watch an old man who has obviously been submerging stalks for many seasons. He carefully finds a place where the water will move easily over the stalks, but not so deep that they can't be retrieved at the right time. The river is low this year, and it takes him a long time to find the right spot. Later in the season, when the retting is complete, the stable fibers will be separated from the stalks and delivered to the mill.

I am amazed to witness an entire village working to produce the dress I am wearing today—from a seed.

—*Jill Vlahos*

beyond death, back to rebirth, what the architect, designer, and author Bill McDonough calls "cradle to cradle." It means making a pair of pants out of infinitely recyclable polyester or a polymer like Nylon 6 and, when it is finally worn out, melting down the pants to a resin and creating another pair from the same resin—over and over again.

No GMO or patented seeds here! Shaking out the hemp stalks to get the seeds for the next planting. Shaanxi Province, China. *Jill Vlahos*

If our future customers are going to send back their pants to us to be recycled when they are no longer usable, then the smart businessman would try to make his pants so they last as long as possible, because you really don't want to see all those pants come back very soon.

In the final analysis, the best effort we can make toward causing no unnecessary harm is to make the best-quality products, ones that are durable, functional, beautiful, and simple.

PRODUCTION PHILOSOPHY

For centuries in Ireland, women hand knit
sweaters for their seafaring husbands. The
bulky, cable-stitched wool was constructed
to ward off harsh elements. Each woman
used a recognizable, family-specific pattern
of stitches, both to reflect love and pride, but
also to be used as a means of identification
if the husband were lost at sea and
his body washed ashore.

—UNKNOWN AUTHOR

Patagonia of course can produce a lot more sweaters than can a single hand knitter working by lamplight in her cottage, on a bluff overlooking the sea. But she has a big advantage over us, a single set of eyes and hands determining the quality of her sweater. The challenge for Patagonia, or for any company serious about making the best product of its kind, is to re-create on an industrial scale the hand knitter's devotion to quality and her ability to keep in mind all the criteria for her final product, a task now spread across several continents in half a dozen companies.

If you decide to make each of your products the best of its kind, you cannot hand off your pattern or blueprint or model to the lowest-bid contractor and expect to get anything close to what you had in mind. When a product has your brand name on it—your "recognizable, family-specific pattern of stitches"—you must work closely and effectively with your suppliers and contractors to replicate that pattern perfectly.

There are six production principles that I've found to be crucial to the faithful execution of our designs.

Involve the Designer with the Producer

When I had my blacksmith shop, I contracted out the tooling of our climbing gear, and some of the production, to Harold Leffler's machine shop in Burbank. Leffler was a draftsman and tool and die maker with fifty years' hands-on experience. We called him the genius as often as we called him Harold. He was so good at his craft that he received requests from aircraft companies around the country to bid on their projects, even though he ran a small shop.

Harold used to joke about the blueprints he received from engineers; they were so overdesigned that the cost to produce them would be ten to twenty times higher than necessary, and in many cases, they would be impossible to make at all. Because I had no training in engineering but did know what I wanted a carabiner or ice screw to do, I would show up with a simple sketch or a carved wooden model, or just an idea in my head, and we would work together to come up with a design that was feasible. Even after Tom Frost, a talented engineer and draftsman, became my partner, we consulted Harold Leffler at all stages of the design process.

My relationship with Leffler taught me how important it is for the designer to work with the producer up front. This applies to every product. Building a house proceeds more smoothly and less expensively when the architect and contractor work out the real-world problems of a blueprint before the cement truck shows up to pour the foundation. Likewise, a rain jacket is better made when the producer understands from the start what the product needs to achieve and, con-

The genius Harold Leffler. C. 1970s.
Tom Frost

versely, when the designer understands what processes have to be followed and, finally, when everyone stays on the job and works as a team until it's done.

Michael Kami refers to this team approach as concurrent, as opposed to assembly-line manufacturing, in which responsibility for one part of the process is handed off in stages to the next in line. A concurrent approach brings all participants together at the beginning of the design phase. As Dr. Kami points out, only about 10 percent of a product's costs are incurred during the design phase, but 90 percent of the costs are irrevocably committed. The ongoing relationship beyond the design phase is critical too. Builders have been known to make on-site changes without knowing the architect's intentions, and sewing contractors can easily compromise a rain jacket's performance by altering construction of a seam to fit their own work habits and practices.

Develop Long-term Relationships with Suppliers and Contractors

Patagonia has never owned a fabric mill or a sewing shop. To make a ski jacket, for instance, we buy fabric from a mill and trims like zippers and facings from other suppliers, and then we contract out the sewing. To work effectively on a single endeavor with so many other companies, with no compromise in product quality, requires a level of mutual commitment much deeper than the traditional business relationship. Mutual commitment requires nurture and trust, and those demand personal time and energy.

Consequently, we do as much business as we can with as few suppliers and contractors as possible. The downside is the risk of becoming highly dependent on another company's performance. But that's exactly the position we want to be in because those companies are also dependent on us. Our potential success is linked. We become like friends, family, mutually selfish business partners; what's good for them is good for us.

Of course you have to choose such relationships carefully. The first thing we look for in a supplier or contractor is the quality of its work. If the standards aren't high already, we don't delude ourselves into thinking they'll be raised for us, no matter how attractive the price. It makes no business sense for a contractor to sew shorts for Costco one day and Patagonia the next. Contractors that sew on the lowest-cost basis wouldn't hire sewing operators of the skill we require or welcome our oversight of their working conditions and environmental standards.

On the other hand, high-quality fabric suppliers and sewing contractors often find us attractive as a business partner. They know that we recognize quality workmanship, skilled employees, and quality working conditions, and we'll pay a fair price. They know, from our reputation, that we'll do our best to establish a long-term relationship, to commit to fabric purchases, and to keep their sewing lines running at an even clip.

When we find a good fit with a supplier or contractor, communication between us has to be as close as it is between departments of our company. Our production department has the responsibility to see that Patagonia's principles, and the specific design aims of each product, are communicated and understood at the mill or at the "needle." Our contract managers must be Patagonia reps in every sense of the word, to convey our standards for product quality, environmental and social concerns, business ethics, and even our image as an outdoor company.

I think of Patagonia as an ecosystem, with its vendors and customers as an integral part of that system. A problem anywhere in the system eventually affects the whole, and this gives everyone an overriding responsibility to the health of the whole organism. It also means that anyone, low on the totem pole or high, inside the company or out, can contribute significantly to the health of the company and to the integrity and value of our products.

Weigh Quality First, Against On-Time Delivery and Low Cost

Every production department of every company has a mandate to deliver a quality product on time and at a reasonable cost. Although it's management's job to treat these three goals as complementary rather than contradictory, what does a company do when it must face a choice?

Patagonia puts quality first, period. A more sales-driven company might sacrifice a degree of quality to achieve on-time delivery, and a mass marketer might sacrifice both quality and on-time delivery to maintain the lowest cost. But if you're committed to making the best products in the world, you can brook no allowance for fabrics that fade on the shelf or zippers that fail or buttons that fall off.

Of course, if you do choose quality *against* on-time delivery or *against* paying a reasonable price, don't pat yourself on the back. You've already blown it. You have to strive constantly to achieve all three, but quality is "more equal."

Go for It, but Do Your Homework

On our road trip to Patagonia in 1968, we stopped to cool off in a jungle river in Colombia. I dived headfirst off the bridge into the coffee-colored water—and planted my head into a sandbar only a foot underwater. I felt a crack and was completely paralyzed, unable even to breathe for a long moment until my senses came back. Later I found that I had suffered a compression fracture of my neck. Well, that was a very risky and stupid act. However, it is possible to accomplish the goal of safely diving into this river, without compromising, if you take the time to learn how to dive off high places carefully and if you plumb the river to see if it's deep enough at the exact spot you plan to dive.

Let me give you a hypothetical scenario. Jane Smith, who is the product line director for sportswear, decides that we have an opportunity to cut a dollar off the cost of our Baggies shorts without compromising on the quality. So production decides to pull them out of the factory where they have been made for years with acceptable quality and put them in a new factory it found in Panama. This seems like a pretty big risk to put 154,000 pairs of Baggies in a factory we have never used before. In fact it's stupid unless we do our homework. So we send people down to check out the factory, see how good the operators are and how they are treated, check out the management to see if it is honest, see if it has the right machines, make sure it understands our quality standards, and then we put our own quality control inspector in the factory during the entire first production run. Under these conditions, would you say the chance of making $150,000 extra profit on this product is worth the risk? I'd say so. Again, like the Zen approach to archery or anything else, you identify the goal and then forget about it and concentrate on the process.

Measure Twice, Cut Once

Let's take a close look at a loose button and the consequences depending on who happens to discover it. Say the button falls off in your customer's hand as she pulls the pants out of the washing machine. Your entire company, and your partners, have failed in the grossest possible way. That hard-earned customer will never again fully trust your claim to quality.

Better for a quality control inspector at your warehouse to make the discovery during a spot check when the goods arrive from the port. Then further checks can be made, and all the pants with loose buttons can be removed from their bags, and the bags from boxes, and all the pants sent over to the sewing room and all the buttons sewn on right, then moved to a staging area and rebagged and reboxed. Better, but expensive; no on-time delivery today.

Better still to spy that loose button at the sewing machine, to work with your contractor to get all the operators to sew the thread through once more because the machines they're using don't lock the stitch properly. Their lines will move a little more slowly, but less harm is done.

Best of all, by far, is to spot the problem with the sewing machine in advance, while you're making the first production sample run. Then you still have lots of options. You might decide, for instance, to purchase five old-fashioned lockstitch machines for the contractor, for which he'll repay you over time on a per unit basis.

That's exactly what we finally did in 1991, though we've suffered through all the other stages too. That suffering taught us that taking extraordinary steps to set up the manufacturing correctly the first time is much cheaper than taking extraordinary steps down the line. If you're committed to being the best, you're going to have to take those extra steps at some point in production anyway. It might as well be at the start.

As this example shows, if you do want to get things right the first time, rigorous specs aren't enough. You have to be a full partner. You have to make sure that your suppliers and contractors have the necessary knowledge and tools to get the job done to your design standards. Getting to that point is not a problem if you and your working partners are mutually committed to the same standards.

Obviously we put a lot of effort into choosing factories that have healthy relationships with their employees. We audit potential partners to determine how they manage workers, we interview workers to determine their perspective on the factory, and we engage civil society to verify that the factory has a positive employment record. But sometimes that doesn't go far enough. Sometimes a factory that has a lot of components of a positive workplace will lack things that are obvious to us but foreign to them, simply because that benefit for workers or that management tool is new or unknown in that region. While it is important to start out working with factories that meet or try to meet our workplace standards, we also have to acknowledge that sometimes our partners need our help. As buyers we have a lot of leverage with a factory, particularly if it is a long-standing partner, with which we have invested a lot of time and energy on quality work or production technology. We have to use that leverage and those relationships to improve working conditions as well as product quality. Doing so is for the good of the entire ecosystem; it's good for workers, good for factories, and good for us. This is an evolving process, and we are continuously learning. Things that we have always done, like screening new factories, are giving way to new ideas like training factory human resources managers to have some of the skills that our own HR team has. Throughout this process we have done what we have done elsewhere in our business; we've begged, borrowed, or stolen the ideas of others. We are a member of the Fair Labor Association, we talk with other companies about their practices, and we ask our factories—and workers—to tell us what kind of help they most need. Most important, we've tried to teach everyone we work with to think the way we do: that the whole supply chain has to be a functioning, interconnected system.

Borrow Ideas from Other Disciplines

Because the world is changing, we can never assume that the way we have done things in the past is adequate for the future. We constantly evaluate the ideas of the moment for improving business processes—from MRP (materials resources plan), to just-in-time, to quick response, to self-managed teams, if we think these approaches may result in a better product delivered on time and at a reasonable cost.

The drive for quality in production in any organization has to go beyond the products themselves. It extends to how we organize ourselves to get a body of work done, how we beg, borrow, and steal good ideas from other companies and cultures, and how we approach the question of the way things are and how they should be. That begins with an attitude of embracing change rather than resisting it. Not just changing without reflection and weighing the relative merits of the new ideas, but nonetheless assuming that if we only look hard enough, there may be a better way to do things.

We should borrow and adapt ideas even from unlikely sources. McDonald's is as far from Patagonia as you can get in its image and many of its values. But one thing it does I respect. No one at McDonald's ever tells a customer, "Sorry, we're all out of iceberg lettuce today." It successfully organizes on-time delivery every day of the week, and I think Patagonia could learn a lesson from McDonald's and the symbiotic relationship it enjoys with its suppliers.

DISTRIBUTION PHILOSOPHY

A clothing company of the size of Patagonia, if it is not diversified in its product line and operations, is as much at risk as a farming operation growing a monocrop. Only the "diseases" are different. Yet very few companies other than Patagonia sell their products at a wholesale level to dealers, sell through their own retail stores, through mail order, and through the Internet, and do it all worldwide. This diversity of distribution has been a tremendous advantage for us. In a recession, when our wholesale sales are down, our direct sales channels do well because there is no lessened demand for our goods from our loyal customers. In the past, recessions have hurt our competitors and driven customers to us because people became less frivolous in their purchases. They didn't mind paying more for goods that won't go out of style and are of such quality that they will last a long time.

Doing business in Japan, Europe, and Canada also buffers us against downturns in the economy in any one of those areas. When Japan's economy was on the rocks in the 1990s, Europe was doing okay. Each means of distribution requires its own expertise and often has demands that conflict with the other channels. The mail-order business requires inventory depth for immediate fulfillment, an intimate knowledge of catalog merchandising, and close analysis of mailing list performance. Selling through the Internet requires constant changing of the Web site. Retail requires well-organized merchandise displays and excellent management and training of floor staff. Traditional wholesale business operates mostly as a

JAPANESE BUSINESS

I've had a great interest in Japanese society since 1964, when I passed through the country on my return from Korea. Much as the Japanese study the West and adopt Western culture and ideas to their advantage, so I have done with theirs. It's a very futuristic society in that the Japanese are always years ahead in how they have had to adapt and to cope with the modern world. Studying Japan gives me a look into the future of all societies that have to face overpopulation, a limited and shrinking resource base, and globalism.

Practically every business book or business school teaches that for a foreign company to do business in Japan, it must seek a partnership or joint venture with a Japanese company. This is especially stressed with the system of distribution, which involves trading companies, banks and jobbers, and all sorts of relationships that no foreign company could hope to finesse on its own.

I had been selling there even before 1975 with Chouinard Equipment, but starting in 1981, Patagonia also tried to break into the Japanese market. We entered in the traditional way, using various trading companies and partnerships. We got nowhere. A trading company that dealt in general sporting goods like baseball bats and fishing gear could hardly be bothered with trying to sell pitons and carabiners.

We tried a partnership with our early climbing packs, but that failed when they put my name and signature on a line of low-end daypacks. Later on we used another manufacturer/distributor that had a similar line of clothing and was mainly interested in controlling our entry into the Japanese market so it wouldn't have to compete with us.

Finally, in 1988, we decided to disregard all the books and go into the Japanese market in our own way. We knew that there was a demand for our clothing because of its quality and that our values were in tune with our Japanese customers. So we went in and started our wholly owned operation. It was going to be an American company doing business California style in Japan. We hired dirtbag Japanese climbers and kayakers; we hired Japanese women for management positions and didn't fire them when they got pregnant. We instituted the Let My People Go Surfing flextime policy. At the time IBM in Japan told us that we were the only American company in the country that was doing it on its own.

What I found out was that Japan is the easiest country in the world to do business in: The laws are straightforward; the government is probusiness; the customs inspectors are intelligent and honest. The reason American companies have had trouble breaking into the Japanese market is that they are trying to do it by the book, and the quality of their products aren't up to Japanese standards.

In a Japanese department store one time I watched a young fellow looking over some shirts. Once he decided he wanted a particular style and size, he went through the entire stack of mediums, looking at the stitching of each shirt until he found the one with the best quality. It was very important for him to walk out of the store knowing he had bought the best shirt in that stock.

We have set the quality standards at Patagonia to meet our most demanding customer, the Japanese. If American car companies had realized that, they could be selling American cars in Japan—if they had also put the steering wheel to the right side.

—Y. C.

Employees of our Kamakura, Japan, headquarters. Not a "salaryman" costume in sight. 2004.
Courtesy of Patagonia

simple distribution business; you bring the merchandise into your warehouse and ship it out.

Few businesses have the confidence to try to master all four business styles, but when you do master them, the four means of distribution work very powerfully in concert. We consider each to be essential to Patagonia's relationship with the customer.

Mail Order

We have always been in the mail-order business, even back in the late 1950s, when the mail was used simply to get pitons from my forge to friends during the winter months, when they couldn't buy directly from the back of my car in Yosemite, the Tetons, or the Canadian Rockies. There was low overhead, no middleman, and no promises that couldn't be kept. Often an order would come, and then the pitons would be forged. Fulfillment was 100 percent.

The mail-order catalog has always been our "soapbox" and enables us to transmit information about Patagonia's philosophies and products directly to people's homes and businesses anywhere in the world. Mail order actively works with our retail stores, dealers, and the international network to support company-wide efforts to develop and retain loyal Patagonia customers.

My first principle of mail order argues that "selling" ourselves and our philosophy is equally important to selling product. Telling the Patagonia story and educating the Patagonia customer on layering systems, on environmental issues, and on the business itself are as much the catalog's mission as is selling the products. This has several practical implications, including how we measure the success of a catalog, how we format the information, and how we allocate space. Above its value as a sales tool, the catalog is first of all an image piece, presenting the company's values and obligations.

Mail order as a means of selling enhances retail, Internet, and wholesale, with all four acting synergistically to serve the customer. The catalog reaches people in their homes with an educational message just as the sales staff in Patagonia's own retail stores, or at dealers' stores, reaches customers firsthand.

Sending a mail-order customer a catalog implies that the product is immediately available. Mail order should fill the demand. Mail-order customers quickly become impatient with out-of-stock situations, particularly early in the season, when they have just received the catalog. They see no reason why they can't have what they want, and they will turn to other companies that *can* deliver. Once they turn to other companies, it is difficult to regain their confidence.

Patagonia's mail-order inventory buy and in-season management are calculated to fulfill orders at 93 to 95 percent throughout the selling season. This rate has been determined to be "ideal" by L. L. Bean and other old-time mail-order houses. To fulfill at a lower rate loses too many sales and customers. To attempt a higher rate leads to inefficient inventory control. In fact you may have to double your inventory to achieve a 98 percent fulfillment rate.

Mail order's mandate (and retail's, for that matter) should be to achieve a 100 percent customer satisfaction rate. That is, give the customer what he wants 100 percent of the time. If a product is out of stock in mail order, the customer service rep takes advantage of the fact that we are a diversified company and pursues other channels to get the product to the customer. Retail managers and customer service reps can pursue one or all of these options:

1. Find the product in one of our retail stores, and have it shipped from there.
2. Find the item in retail, wholesale, or closeout inventory.
3. Locate the item in one of our dealers' shops, and let the dealer make the sale, thereby making two customers happy.

THE ENVIRONMENTAL COST OF TRANSPORTATION

Our environmental assessment program showed us that the single greatest use of energy in the life span of a product is transportation. For example, a Patagonia shirt requires roughly 110,000 BTUs of energy to manufacture, from acquiring raw materials to making the fabric to sewing a finished shirt. Shipping that item air freight from Ventura to Boston, in a package with eighteen other shirts, takes another 50,000 BTUs per shirt. In other words, it takes half again as much fossil fuel energy to move it once than it did to make it.

This brings up several considerations. One, we should be producing locally whenever possible.

Two, consumers should not be ordering items to be shipped by airfreight simply because it's convenient, especially if it's a box of lobsters from Maine or a fresh salad from California. The dollar cost added to the item may be relatively small, but the environmental cost is huge.

Third, it becomes apparent that the global economy is not sustainable. It's completely dependent on burning up cheap fossil fuel. Shipping goods by rail or by boat uses 400 BTUs per ton for each mile shipped. Truck freight uses more than 3,300 BTUs per ton, and air cargo uses 21,670 BTUs, to move a ton of goods one mile.

When shopping long distance by catalog or on the Internet, you should reconsider ordering that live lobster from Maine, and ask yourself if you really need that pair of pants sent overnight or by second-day air.

—Y. C.

The customer should have to make only one phone call. Just as the Patagonia production philosophy requires on-time product delivery from its suppliers, so Patagonia must deliver its products on time to its customers, and "on time" means *when the customer wants it.*

Our model for customer service is the old-fashioned hardware store owner who knows his tools and what they're made for. His idea of service is to wait on a customer until the customer finds the right widget for the job, no matter how long it takes. At the other end of the spectrum is the employee who doesn't follow through, as the letter quoted below illustrates. It came from our manager in Japan in 1989 as an explanation of the lengths he had to go to in order to make up for bad customer service by one of his employees.

> A woman did request our catalog and paid 600 yen ($4.00 US) to us, but Patagonia Japan staff lost her address and phone number in messy desk and office. After two weeks husband of woman made phone call and he was so angry like volcano. He entirely refused excuse of staff. He needed talk-fight with Mr. Responsibility of Patagonia Japan. He said, "You guys lie, just take money and never send catalog. Hey, this is your way? I am working legally to stop your business with the public facility." I decided to take train to Tokyo from Yokohama to hand catalog and apologize directly to him. However, volcano-angry customer additionally said, "Even if you come to me and my wife I will never stop to kill your business." At his home, he needed my begging head on the floor (this is biggest humility of Samurai). The customer was impressed with my behavior and he said, "Thank you for your delivery and your mind." There are not so many customer like this in Japan, but he is not special type of Japanese customer, he is pretty usual customer if problem happened.
>
> *Katsumi Fujikura*

Good customer service of course would have provided the woman her catalog when she asked for it.

Even though mail order is the most scientific or "formulaic" of the Patagonia distribution channels, our first rule of mail order is to break the rules of mail order that don't apply to us. As a start-up or ongoing business, mail order is the most predictable. Some of the classic mail-order rules make as much sense for Patagonia as for any other mail-order business, others do not. Some rules that other mail-order businesses follow and Patagonia *does not* are:

1. Conduct a square-inch sales analysis of the catalog page.
   This is irrelevant and even damaging to our image.
2. Consult focus groups for direction.
   We ask ourselves.
3. Give more expensive items more space.
   Our socks sometimes get as much space as our guide jacket.
4. Write copy that appeals to vanity, greed, or guilt.
   Our copy pretty much sticks to facts and philosophy.

Since the publication of the 1972 Chouinard Equipment catalog that contained the "Clean Climbing" essay we have seen that the primary purpose of our catalogs is to serve as a vehicle to communicate with our customers—whether it is by trying to change climbing philosophy, by rallying them to register and vote for the environment, as we did in 2004, or by just relating stories. Then, by the way, after we have achieved that purpose, we present the products they can buy.

Over the years we have come upon a balance we find just about ideal: 55 percent product content and 45 percent devoted to message—essays, stories, and image photos. Whenever we have edged that content toward increased product presentation, we have actually experienced a decrease in sales.

Internet

Being a confirmed Luddite all my life and a nonuser of computers, I never could have imagined that the Internet would become such an important part of our business. Yet it is the one place our customers are going to more and more to look for information about the company's brand, products, history, service, and image. Our Internet business runs by the same values and philosophy as mail order. The difference is that it can react more quickly to the needs of the company and the customers. For instance, at the end of a season we can post our closeout sale items and be selling them on the same day. Or we can rally our customers to an environmental crisis. In 2003–04 our customers sent out fifteen thousand letters to the president of the United States, asking him to act on taking out the four dams on the Snake River that are key to restoring salmon to that river system.

The Web site can be a very big tool to talk to many or something that can be personalized when appropriate. For example, e-mails sent out from the Web site are sometimes based on how cold it is in different parts of the country with different clothing system ideas for customers.

The Web is different in another way from mail order: It requires an individual to keep clicking and moving through the Web site. It is not like a catalog that can be flipped through passively.

Our Internet sales now exceed our mail-order sales, and its success can be attributed to the synergy of Patagonia's being in the other three methods of distribution. Customers can view the quality of our products in a dealer's or our own stores, or see them in our catalog, and they can feel assured that what they order from their fuzzy little computer screen will be of the quality they expect.

Retail

There are several historical reasons for Patagonia's entrance into the retail arena. The specialty outdoor market in the sixties and seventies still consisted mostly of hard goods, and the bulk of time and money was spent on advertising those goods. Those shop owners who chose to venture into clothing did so in a small way, cherry-picking the available lines. You hoped to catch a trend, not market a line and take a risk. No single Patagonia dealer carried more than 25 percent of the line. Merchandising was an unknown concept, and display was done on a sea of chrome racks. Nothing was folded, and our clothes were mixed in with other brands throughout the stores. In some cases, our underwear was thrown into big cardboard boxes on the floor. Buyers were also afraid to buy clothes or colors that deviated from the "safe" red or blue.

The industry needed a change, and we didn't see anyone trying to establish order out of the chaos. In 1973 we owned a small retail store in Ventura, but we didn't know any more about display and merchandising than did the other stores, so we couldn't very well tout our ideas unless we could talk from experience. We needed a direct link with our customer, a place to try merchandising ideas and new products.

At the time Berkeley was the hub of the outdoor industry, so we looked for a store location in the Bay Area. We figured what worked there would work for the country as a whole. In North Beach in San Francisco we found a building we loved, a garage built in 1924, with great natural lighting and a garden out back. Local friends tried to discourage us because the location had no dedicated parking and was off the beaten path for shopping. But we thought our customers would come to us, and rather than pay high rent in a well-trafficked location, we preferred to put the money into renovating this old garage and make it into a beautiful destination store. We designed our own racks and shelving. We displayed most of the

PHILOSOPHY OF ARCHITECTURE

The philosophy of clothing design is really no different from that for other products, including buildings. The following are guidelines we use in creating a new retail store or office building that will optimize aesthetics, function, and responsibility.

1. Don't build a new building unless it's absolutely necessary. The most responsible thing to do is to buy used buildings, construction materials, and furniture.
2. Try to save old or historic buildings from being torn down. Any structural changes should honor the historical integrity of the building. We rectify misguided "improvements" made by previous tenants and strip away fake modern facades, ending up we hope with a building that is a "gift to the neighborhood."
3. If you can't be retro, build quality. The aesthetic life expectancy of the building should be as long as the physical material's life span.
4. Use recycled, and recyclable, materials like steel girders, studs, remilled wood, and straw bales. Install fixtures from waste materials like pressed sunflower hulls and agricultural waste.
5. Anything that is built should be repairable and easily maintained.
6. Buildings should be constructed to last as long as possible, even if this initially involves a higher price.
7. Each store must be unique. The heroes, sports, history, and natural features of each area should be reflected and honored.

—Y. C.

clothes folded rather than hung and worked out our chromatic scheme to get the most "pop" from the color. We blew up image shots from the catalog and hung them on the walls.

The San Francisco store is still our favorite. It is recycled and has the authentic architecture and construction of the 1920s California craftsman.

Ex-auto shop. The San Francisco store in North Beach.
Courtesy of Patagonia

After our success in San Francisco, we thought Seattle was a prime location for another store. The market was undersold to dealers who carried only a small depth of the line. The nineteen dealers in the Seattle-Tacoma area in total were selling less Patagonia goods than was our one store in Ventura. There were plenty of "users" and a population base to support two million dollars in sales. During the first three years after the Seattle store opened, in November 1987, wholesale sales to the area dealers increased an average of 21 percent annually. Obviously we were not stealing business from our dealers because we were undersold in that area, and our being successful with our own retail store gave confidence to our dealers that they too could sell more Patagonia goods.

After that we decided to go international. I'd spent a lot of time climbing in the Alps in the 1960s, especially in the French Alps around Chamonix, camping in the mud in Snell's field and drinking an occasional beer at the Bar National. Chamonix is the most cosmopolitan of the Alpine towns, with as many German, Italian, Scandinavian, British, and American climbers and skiers as French. I had fond memories of my time there and believed it was an ideal place to showcase the Patagonia line and create a direct relationship with a wide range of European customers. I wanted to create a local hangout, staffed with international hard-core skiers and climbers. I also wanted it to be a center for environmental activism, responsible for cleaning garbage off the glaciers and opposing the polluting truck traffic through the Mont Blanc tunnel.

When Roger McDivitt went to Chamonix on vacation in 1986, Malinda, who was now running the retail sector of Patagonia, asked him to look around for a building to rent. A week later an excited Roger called to say he had found the perfect space. He'd even signed a lease! When the photos arrived via express mail, Malinda, who had run the San Francisco remodeling project, sat down and cried. Then she blew up the photos on the copy machine and traced the horrible 1950s Euro-modern facade. She stripped away the orange louver trim to bare the structure and then superimposed some of the classic trim shapes from photos of neighboring, older Chamonix buildings. Eventually we had a store all Chamonix could be proud of. Malinda, a zealot, insists that any building we occupy must honor its surrounding history and culture and must be prepared to last another hundred years.

Before renovation of
the Chamonix store.
Courtesy of Patagonia

After renovation.
Courtesy of Patagonia

Wholesale

The main benefit of a wholesale operation is that it requires a much smaller investment to reach customers than mail order or our own retail stores. Wholesale reaches potential customers where they live, travel, and shop for their hard goods, and it places the labor and expense of selling to the customer on the dealer's shoulders. The dealer has control over the relationship with the customer, and the dealer then becomes the voice of Patagonia. So how do we ensure that the real Patagonia "story" isn't lost in translation?

The way to get our message across is to develop a partnership with our dealers. The partnership we seek with dealers is similar to that which our product development and production staffs seek with vendors and contractors. The only difference is that in this case Patagonia wholesale is the supplier. Why should we want to put in the effort to develop these partnerships with dealers when it requires much more time, energy, and fortitude than does the traditional semiannual "buffalo hunt" for new dealers, where it seems far easier just to open one or two hundred new dealers every year and just get rid of the ones that don't work out?

There are key benefits to having a working partnership with a few good dealers:

1. We don't have to expend the effort, time, and money to seek out new dealers.
2. We limit our credit risks.
3. We minimize the legal problems associated with cutting off a dealer whose bad service is a reflection on us.
4. We develop loyal buyers who make a commitment to the line and either carry a broad representation of the line or, in the case of a small specialty shop, in-depth inventory.

5. We maintain better control over our product and image.

6. We receive better information about the market and our products.

Our dealers also have advantages in this kind of relationship. They are:

1. A product line that sells year after year.

2. Protection from market saturation.

3. A stable pricing structure.

4. Expertise from us in buying, merchandising, and displaying our products.

5. Being part of Patagonia's synergistic marketing and distribution program.

In its earliest days Patagonia had no trouble focusing. We knew whom to sell to: any store in the country that sold Chouinard Equipment for alpinists (which in 1974 established two qualifications for dealership: minimum sales of a thousand dollars per year and a floor staff that included at least one climber). We knew what to sell; the original line consisted of the rugby shirt, sailor shirt, Stand Up Shorts, and the Chamonix Guide Sweater. And we had a simple, shared strategy with our dealers: Sell as much as possible.

The dealer in turn had to consider Patagonia a genuine partner, and this involves more than trust and goodwill. As a rule in the United States we work to have eventually 20 to 25 percent of a dealer's business and/or be its first- or second-largest clothing vendor. This establishes a de facto partnership. Even a dealer with a strong ego who "did it my way" will listen to someone who supplies 20 to 25 percent of what she sells.

Usually a prospective dealer will want to know why and how establishing a mutual strategy with us will benefit his business. He will want to know how it will improve sales, attract new customers, and increase the loyalty of existing ones. It should be noted here that a dealer that is a partner has to be a full and *contributing* partner. There is no such thing as a canned or turnkey Patagonia merchandising program. Such a program loses its life and momentum the minute the rep walks out the door. We work most successfully with the dealer who invests time, energy, and thought into tailoring a Patagonia program to her store or customers and who welcomes our continuing participation and makes use of our expertise.

In 1985 I gave a speech about the gloomy state of the specialty outdoor industry:

> Let's look at what's been happening to retail in general in America and how it's changing. Take groceries as an example. It used to be that to put dinner on the table, you had to visit a bakery, a butcher or fishmonger, a general grocer, and a green grocer for vegetables and fruits. Then along came the supermarket where, under one roof, you could buy bread, meat, vegetables, milk, and whatever. The supermarket was great for Middle America in the fifties to the seventies, when people were satisfied with white bread, fish sticks, and hamburger. But times are changing. Now people have shopping lists that read like an international food fair. Take my own the other day: wasabe, fresh albacore, basmati rice, chayotes, and kimchi! I know of a store being built in Marin County that will be a full-on organic supermarket with no product in the store with dangerous or chemical additives. No hormones in the meat, no preservatives in the bread, and a full-time chemist in a lab in house to check on the produce. There will be a bakery with all whole grain goods and a deli with all sorts of prepared foods to take out like Zabar's or Dean & DeLuca in New York. These people know what your average Marin County customer's needs are, and they plan to service him. For the average eclectic customer living

in a not so futuristic place as California, shopping for good food has gotten back to going to the fish market, the health food store, the bakery, and the butcher's for nonprepackaged meat and no hormone chicken.

So how does this compare with the evolution of retail in the outdoor industry? The first specialty outdoor shops were hardware stores specializing in climbing gear like Gerry's and Holubar. For ski gear there was The Ski Hut in Berkeley, and of course for sailing there were chandleries selling varnish and nuts and bolts. And then came the backpacking boom of the sixties and seventies. You could get everything you needed to climb or backpack from one of three hundred backpacking shops in the U.S. Backpacking and climbing peaked as sports in 1972–73, and business in the hardware (meaning sleeping bags, tents, ropes, etc.) started declining. At about this time Chouinard/Patagonia was one of the companies responsible for talking dealers into going soft—that is, putting their dollars into lifestyle clothing. So now in the eighties we have a situation a bit like the Middle American supermarket. Under one roof of your typical outdoor shop you can buy some rugged outdoor clothes, some kayaking and climbing gear, and high-quality sleeping bags, but it's a bit like the white bread and fish sticks syndrome. You won't find an eighty-degree dihedral slalom kayak paddle or overboots for expedition or winter climbing. They can special order it, but it will take six to eight weeks. Climbing gear? Oh, it's nailed onto the wall behind the sleeping bags. They *do* have a five-hundred-dollar tent that's similar to a Eureka knockoff you can buy at the fishing and hunting store for two hundred dollars. And if you want a certain piece of Patagonia clothing, there's probably a 10 percent chance it will be in stock. You see what's happened? By carrying a little bit of this and a little of that, these stores have evolved into nonspecialty stores. That would be okay if your average outdoor store customer had average tastes and average mentality. But we are talking about smart people with money and not much free time. If there is one common trait to all outdoor people, it's the fact that they do not spend their free time aimlessly shopping. If he or she is going to drive for twenty minutes to a store, it's to buy certain needed items; it's not to be entertained like the Bloomingdale's customer. And I can tell you these people are going to be pretty angry if the store doesn't have what they want. In most cases the consumer has far outgrown the capabilities of the average outdoor store to service him. He is being forced into buying through mail order. Or he will shop at REIs and other bigger stores that offer a larger selection. Even the more progressive department stores are doing a better job of merchandising and selling lifestyle clothes like rugby shirts and down jackets. The little specialty shop doesn't have enough space or inventory to be a clothing store and often no longer has the expertise to be a good climbing or backpacking store. By and large we have a no-growth industry with some larger and more progressive shops doing well, but the majority of the shops are not going anywhere.

What happened since I gave that talk twenty years ago paints an even gloomier picture for the majority of small retailers. The generation of climbers and skiers and fly fishermen who started these specialty stores in the sixties and seventies are burned out and either have retired or are ready to. Their kids don't want to take over, and since the industry is no longer in a growth mode, there are no buyers in sight. The REIs, Sportmarts, and Decathlons (in France) are taking even bigger chunks of the business. With mainstream companies like Ralph Lauren, Tommy Hillfiger, and Nike all making Gore-Tex shells and down jackets, you really can outfit yourself for Everest in Macy's department store, and with a black and yellow one-piece snowmobile suit from Costco you will be better equipped than Edmund Hillary was in 1953.

Since Patagonia has no desire to sell to department stores or to the giant sporting goods chains, our dealer list has gone down 40 percent since 1985. It's not a healthy situation for the specialty outdoor industry, yet the problems and the solutions are no different for all small retail stores worldwide that are facing competition from the Wal-Marterization of retail.

There's a wine shop in Portland, Oregon, called 750ml that is a good example of how one shop competes with the big liquor and wine stores. Since it is a small store, the owner has personally chosen every bottle of wine. A customer like me who likes an "earthy" flavor in red wines but is too cheap to go for a great French Bordeaux can explain to a knowledgeable salesperson what he's looking for and be guided to just the right bottle and be told how long he has to cellar the wine to optimize that "barnyard" flavor he's looking for.

One of my favorite fly shops and Patagonia dealers is Blue Ribbon Flies in West Yellowstone, Montana, a small town with four other full-service fly shops. Blue Ribbon is a small shop with not a big choice of rods and reels and gear, just enough so there is everything you need to fish the Yellowstone waters.

All its flies are made in the United States by thirty of the best flytiers in the country. During the fishing season there are two tiers on the floor who will custom tie any fly you want. A fly shop that doesn't carry fly-tying materials is not a fly shop as far as I'm concerned. This shop not only has a great selection but collects and dyes a lot of the hair and feathers itself. It will even offer to dye a customer's pheasant skin purple if that's asked for. It donates 2 percent of its net sales to conservation causes around Yellowstone Park, and it gets mail-order customers from across the country who will buy a seven-hundred-dollar rod from them because they know that fourteen dollars of that purchase will help create better fishing for them the next time they visit the area. Blue Ribbon's business has tripled over the last seven years.

There's no secret to running a great retail store. It just requires hard work and great customer service.

IMAGE PHILOSOPHY

Even if he or she isn't aware of it, every individual spends an entire lifetime creating and evolving a personal image that others perceive. A company too creates and evolves an image that can stem from its reason to be in business, can grow out of its actions, or perhaps is assembled from pieces by the creative mind of an advertising person. A company's (and a person's) image can be very different from their self-image.

Patagonia's image arises directly from the values, outdoor pursuits, and passions of its founders and employees. While it has practical and nameable aspects, it can't be made into a formula. In fact, because so much of the image relies on authenticity, a formula would destroy it. Ironically, part of Patagonia's authenticity lies in not being concerned about having an image in the first place. Without a formula, the only way to sustain an image is to live up to it. Our image is a direct reflection of who we are and what we believe.

What's at the heart of the Patagonia image? How are we perceived by the public? Foremost, certainly, is our origin as a blacksmith shop that made the best climbing hardware in the world. The beliefs, attitudes, and values of those free-thinking, independent climbers and surfers who worked there became the basis for Patagonia's culture, and from that culture evolved an image: authentic, hard-core, quality products made by the same people who used them.

Our image has evolved to include the culture of a new generation of climbers, kayakers, fishermen, and surfers who make the best outdoor clothing in the world.

Water Girl ambassador Maureen Drummey
in Costa Rica. *David Pu'u*

At the heart is their commitment to
wildness, both in the natural world
and in the sports they serve. They
continue to hold to certain values and beliefs that were inherent in the fledgling
company of the 1950s but have brought with them another, a willingness to take
strong stands on environmental issues.

The fact that we make clothing for a multitude of outdoor uses has been a great
advantage to us. We have a greater expanded future than if we made clothing for
just one market, like our original line for mountain climbing. But we also have recognized that we should not attempt to do it all under one brand.

The Water Girl USA line of women's water sports–inspired clothing was not
brought baring the Patagonia label because it was too much of a stretch to imag-

ine a product like Patagonia bikinis. It would be like L. L. Bean's coming out with snowboards; it wouldn't work. Water Girl kept all the values of its parent company, Patagonia, but was given its own name and allowed to develop its own style, identity, and image. It is also run by active women who make what they want to wear themselves.

Patagonia's image is a human voice. It expresses the joy of people who love the world, who are passionate about their beliefs, and who want to influence the future. It is not processed; it won't compromise its humanity. This means that it will offend, and it will inspire.

It's important to control our image—not only through the actions we take, the products we sell, and living up to our past but by how we are perceived through the normal business channels of marketing and selling our products. I've divided this aspect into four areas.

Telling the Entire Story

Many companies communicate with their customers primarily through advertising. This grabs your attention but can't hold it. A quick glance, and you're back to the article you were reading or the show you were watching or on to someone else's ad or the mute button. It is said that a TV viewer has to be hit on the head with the same ad seven or eight times before it begins to register.

Just as Patagonia makes products for a deeper, less distracted experience of the world and its wild places, our image has to convey refuge from, and offer an alternative to, a virtual world of fast-moving, mind-skimming (and -numbing) pictures and sound. In order to tell our whole story, we need the customer's undivided attention. That can be done these days through a Web site or a catalog. We have both, and there is an art and a science to each. A Web site allows the mouse-armed customer to explore more quickly and easily his areas of strong interest. A catalog has the advantage of self-containment and mobility, of not confining the customer's experience of Patagonia to a computer, of providing surprises as the customer turns the page.

The first goal of the catalog is to share and encourage a particular philosophy of life, of what undergirds the image. The basic tenets of that philosophy are: a deep appreciation for the environment and a strong motivation to help solve the environmental crisis; a passionate love for the natural world; a healthy skepticism toward authority; a love for difficult, human-powered sports that require practice and mastery; a disdain for motorized sports like snowmobiling or jet skiing; a bias for whacko, often self-deprecating humor; a respect for real adventure (defined best as a journey from which you may not come back alive—and certainly not as the same person); a taste for real adventure; and a belief that less is more (in design and in consumption).

The catalog is our bible for each selling season. Every other medium we use to tell our story—from the Web site, to hang tags, to retail displays, to press releases to videos—builds from the catalog's base and from its pictorial and editorial standards.

Photography

Looking back at the early Patagonia catalogs, I find it really embarrassing to see how "corny" the photos look. The clothes were shown on people, and since we couldn't afford real models or professional photographers, we used our friends, put them in stupid poses, and snapped a photo. Pretty bad, but that's what everyone else's catalog or advertising looked like in those days.

One day while I was out surfing with my friend Rick Ridgeway, an idea popped into my head. I told him that I was going to start photographing the clothes without the people in them and we were going to collect photos from our customers

Friends and neighbors modeling bunting jackets in the 1980 catalog. Ironically, the camel-colored bunting jacket she is wearing was being offered on Japanese eBay in 2005 for four thousand dollars. *Rick Ridgeway*

Laurie Mastrella casting for silver salmon, Lake Creek, Alaska. *Rex Bryngelson*

From the very beginning of our catalog, we have always tried to portray women as equal to men. When we showed women climbing, they were leading, not following. This photo of ambassador Lynn Hill in 1983 says it all.
Rick Ridgeway

of real people doing real things. We put a notice in our catalog for our customers to "capture a Patagoniac." We were inundated with photo submissions from our customers and photographers, and we had to create a photo department with Rick's wife, Jennifer, as manager and editor.

A photo of a real climber with a name on a real rock climb and showing a little skin can be a lot sexier than a half-naked nameless New York model posing as a climber. Plus it's more honest, and honesty is what we strive for in our marketing and photography. So we're careful about the images we select.

That means we reject lots of photos. We don't slip a pile jacket onto a Bantu chief for a photo op unless it's really his jacket. That's condescending. We don't print shots of sallow-skinned backpackers trudging over the Appalachian Trail on an autumn weekend. That's too safe. We don't show jut-jawed mountaineers planting a flag atop a windswept peak. That's too conquistadorial.

We have shown, and do show, climbers picnicking on the hood of a rusted Chevy at the base of a climb, travelers debarking from *African Queen* boats, a gone-to-seed fishing cabin in Belize, a euphoric skier rising from a face plant in fresh powder, a Galápagos tortoise tearing apart a pile jacket by a tent-side laundry, a sculpture made of trash on a glacier above Chamonix, weary sailors under deck on a Transpac boat, a mechanic greasing a ball joint under a road-worn truck, a marine biologist banding a bird in the field, Julia Butterfly Hill guarding her redwood, and skiers at a back bowl camp "watching" an ice sculpture TV.

Copy

From the days of Chouinard Equipment, our copy standards have been

Ambassador Steph Davis, making the first female ascent of Pink Flamingo, Utah, desert.
Eric Perlman

high. Since we've always been different, it's been even more important that we tell our own story clearly. We have always used text to argue ideas as well as sell products. We have two basic kinds of copy: personal stories that illustrate one of our values or promote a cause and descriptive copy that sells products.

The "Clean Climbing" essay in the 1972 Chouinard Equipment catalog not only encouraged climbers to climb "clean" but also was the first piece ever written about how to use the new chocks. As a result, Chouinard Equipment's piton business dried up, and its chock business exploded, nearly overnight. To show its impact, far beyond a business tool, that catalog was reviewed as a mountaineering book in the *American Alpine Journal*. A 1991 introductory essay, "Reality Check," reminded customers that every product we make causes environmental harm and encouraged people to buy better and to buy less.

Patagonia catalogs have printed "field reports," brief essays about experiences in the wild, by writers and friends like Paul Theroux, Tom Brokaw, Gretel Ehrlich, Rick Ridgeway, and Terry Tempest Williams. We have commissioned and printed environmental essays by, among others, Bill McKibben, Vandana Shiva, Sue Halpern, Carl Safina, and Jared Diamond. Even our regular product copywriters have impressive credentials. Ellen Meloy was a finalist in 2003 for a Pulitzer Prize for her nonfiction book *The Anthropology of Turquoise*.

Some stories are easier to tell, more readily apparent or immediate than others. If you were to tell a parent that the local drinking water is unsafe for their children, you'd spark immediate outrage. But tell the same person that cancer clusters show up inexplicably in long-term studies of children who live in their pesticide-intensive farming community, and the response is less pronounced. That story is emotionally less immediate, and it requires more effort and depth in the telling.

Product copy provides the necessary facts about fabric detail and usage and also supports some of the subtler points made in the photographs about what we wish for in sports and in life. Our accuracy standards are very high. Since we don't mind taking a stand or risk giving offense, there's all the more reason to get the facts right.

As for style, we write as though we were the customers. In fact, since we are still some of our own best customers, this is not too difficult. We don't speak to what is perceived as the lowest common denominator. We speak to each customer as we want to be treated, as an engaged, intelligent, trusted individual.

Promotion

We have three general guidelines for all promotional efforts by Patagonia, both within and beyond the pages of the catalog:

1. Our charter is to inspire and educate rather than promote.
2. We would rather earn credibility than buy it. The best resources for us are the word-of-mouth recommendation from a friend or favorable comments in the press.
3. We advertise only as a last resort.

Ideally, every great product would sell itself. Some products do just that. We've sold our polo shirts for twenty years, and we've never advertised them. Nor do we give them much space in the catalog, except to show off the variety of new colors. I wish all our products could stand on their own like polo shirts or Baggies.

We make certain assumptions about our customers, not just that they are intelligent. We assume that they don't shop as entertainment, that they're not out to "buy a life," that they want to deepen and simplify, not junk up, their lives, and that they are fed up with or indifferent to being targets for aggressive advertising. We know that for customers as well as for ourselves, the most valued advice we

Soul surfer, shaper, snowboarder, and ambassador for Patagonia Gerry Lopez. *Kirk Devoll*

can receive is that from a trusted friend. After that, we respect the opinions of pros or experts like outdoor instructors, climbing guides, fishing guides, or river outfitters.

The pros live and work in their clothing every day. For this reason, we have always offered a pro purchase program selling clothes at a discount to key people in various technical markets. We work with a variety of groups, from ski patrols at challenging areas like Jackson Hole and Telluride, to river guides in the Grand Canyon, to climbers off to attempt the Trango Towers in Pakistan, to groups working on environmental issues, people working to reintroduce wolves to Yellowstone or Greenpeace activists.

We also provide gear, and sometimes stipends, to top climbers, surfers, and endurance athletes to wear our clothes, in order to give us feedback and help with design issues. They advise our retail staff on how to sell our technical sports-specific products, attend sales meetings, and generally serve as ambassadors for the company. This reflects well on Patagonia at trade shows or consumer events and helps create trickle-down word of mouth. We do draw lines with this policy. They aren't paid, for instance, according to the number of cover shots they get wearing clothes with our logo.

Sponsorship of famous athletes is a good promotional tool for selling to kids who dream someday of being able to surf like Kelly Slater or climb like Chris Sharma, but I think sponsorship hurts soul sports like surfing or climbing. As I wrote in an article for *Climbing* magazine, "Sponsorship . . . by the outdoor industry is a no-win situation for the climber in the long run. Being paid to climb forces one to compromise one's values: it encourages the alpine climber to seek routes that make good press, and it can force an otherwise wonderfully eccentric sport climber to act out a role in order to become more sellable in the media." I also think sponsorship hurts companies in the long run by tying the company image to an ephemeral career or to a single person who often has nothing to do with your product or service. (What does Hertz think of its years with O. J. Simpson these days?)

On the other hand, the more independent the outsider who praises your company or products, the greater the credibility. Talking about ourselves to our parents on the phone is fine, but in every other situation the word from outside carries more weight.

Editorial coverage is also important. Public relations companies tell you that a favorable, independent press notice is worth three to eight times the same space paid for with an advertisement. Using a more conservative one-to-one formula, we calculated that in 1994, the year we came out with Synchilla fleece made from recycled soda bottles, we generated five-million-dollars' worth of free press for the company.

Our approach to public relations is aggressive: If we have a news angle, we play it. We work hard to bring our stories to reporters, whether about new products, our stands on environmental issues, or our child care program. But we don't produce glossy PR kits or throw elaborate press parties at trade shows. We believe the best way to get press is to have something to say.

Advertising, as I mentioned, rates dead last as a credible source of information. What works best for us are paid announcements for a new store opening or to create environmental awareness of a specific issue—e.g., the reasons to demolish a dam on a particular river. We do occasionally use advertising to support the brand, usually in small-circulation sport specialty magazines. Overall, we do far less advertising (usually less than 1 percent of sales) than most outdoor companies, let alone clothing companies. In advertising, the impression has to be quick and timely, but all our usual standards for photography and copy apply. The photo in the Patagonia ad is often the best in the magazine.

Foto di Groupo of some of our ambassadors. 2004.
Jeff Johnson

FINANCIAL PHILOSOPHY

Who are businesses really responsible
to? Their customers? Shareholders?
Employees? We would argue that it's
none of the above. Fundamentally,
businesses are responsible to their
resource base. Without a healthy
environment there are no
shareholders, no employees, no
customers and no business.
—From a series of ads we did in 2004

We are a product-driven company. That means the product comes first and the company exists to create and support our products. This is different from a distribution company whose product may not be the primary concern but rather service.

When you look closely at some companies, it may be a surprise to find that not all of them are in business to produce a tangible product or service. The real product may be the company itself, which is just being grown to be sold one day.

In a public corporation the product may be the stock, because all decisions made by the CEO and other internal stockholders, or by holders of options on stock and the board of directors (also stockholders), are made not for the long-term health of the corporation but to keep the stock price up until the principals can cash out. This can lead to "cooking the books," which is often the only way to show "profits" or growth every quarter, and it leads to confusion in the company about why it's in business.

Our mission statement says nothing about making a profit. In fact Malinda and I consider our bottom line to be the amount of good that the business has accomplished over the year. However, a company needs to be profitable in order to stay in business and to accomplish all its other goals, and we do consider profit to be a vote of confidence, that our customers approve of what we are doing.

The third part of our mission statement, "using business to implement and inspire solutions to the environmental crisis," puts the responsibility of leadership directly on us. If we wish to lead corporate America by example, we have to be profitable. No company will respect us, no matter how much money we give away or how much publicity we receive for being one of the "100 Best Companies," if we are not profitable. It's okay to be eccentric, as long as you are rich; otherwise you're just crazy.

At Patagonia, making a profit is not *the* goal because the Zen master would say profits happen "when you do everything else right." In our company, finance consists of much more than the management of money. It is primarily the art of leadership through the balancing of traditional financing approaches in a business that is anything but traditional. In many companies, the tail (finance) wags the dog (corporate decisions). We strive to balance the funding of environmental activities with the desire to continue in business for the next hundred years.

Our philosophy does not hold that finance is the root of all business. Rather, it complements all other segments of the company. We recognize that our profits are directly tied to the quality of our work and our product. A company that doesn't take quality seriously will attempt to maximize profits by cost cutting, increasing sales by creating an artificial demand for the goods, and hammering the rank and file to work harder.

In direct sales distribution you do not necessarily make more money by cramming more product into your catalog pages or onto your retail sales floor. A quality presentation will always outsell "messiness." We recognize that we make the most profit by selling to our loyal customers. A loyal customer will buy new products with little sales effort and will tell all his friends. A sale to a loyal customer is worth six to eight times more to our bottom line than a sale to another customer.

We believe that quality is no longer a luxury. It is sought out by the consumer, and it is expected. For example, the Strategic Planning Institute has been collecting data for years on the performance of thousands of companies. It publishes a yearly report, titled PIMS (Profit Impact of Market Strategy). That report has begun to show quite clearly that *quality*, not price, has the highest correlation with business success. In fact the institute has found that overall, companies with high product and service quality reputations have on average return-on-investment rates twelve times higher than their lower-quality and lower-priced competitors.

Environmental concerns also influence our financial decisions. In the mid-nineties we decided to change the packaging of our thermal underwear. We were using a thick, wraparound cardboard header inside a heavy Ziploc plastic bag. To get away from this packaging for the heavier-weight expedition underwear, we decided to go without any packaging at all and hang them up like regular clothing. As for the underwear made of lighter-weight material, we just rolled them up and put a rubber band around them. We were warned to be prepared for a 30 percent cut in sales because we were competing with companies that were extremely competitive with their packaging. One competitor, for example, put its product out in adorable sealed tin cans. We did it anyway because it was the right thing to do. The first year this practice kept twelve tons of material from being shipped around the world and eventually being discarded and dumped into landfills, and it saved the company $150,000 in unnecessary packaging. It also brought us a 25 percent increase in thermal underwear sales. Since they weren't hidden away in a package and had to be displayed like the regular clothing, people could feel the material and appreciate the quality. And since they were displayed like the other clothes, we were forced to make our underwear look like regular clothing, to the point that now most Capilene underwear tops can be worn as a regular shirt, fulfilling our goal of making clothes that are multifunctional.

Returns and bad quality in manufacturing cost millions of dollars each year (we know that in 1988 each return cost us an average of twenty-six dollars to process, and that number has only gone up). But what is the cost of a dissatisfied customer? Recently a worldwide survey of customers found that only 14 percent of Americans were likely to contact a company about a problem. In Europe the number was less than 8 percent, and in Japan only 4 percent. Correspondingly, other studies show that one-half to one-third of customers who have had problems will never purchase from that company again.

We are a privately owned company, and we have no desire to sell the company or to sell stock to outside investors, and we don't want to be financially leveraged. In addition, we have no desires to expand Patagonia beyond the specialty outdoor market. So how does finance react to these very clear-cut dictates?

First of all, by growing only at a "natural rate." When our customers tell us they are frustrated by not being able to buy our products because of constant out-of-stock situations, then we need to make more, and that leads to "natural growth." We do not create artificial demand for our goods by advertising in *Vanity Fair* or GQ or on buses in inner cities, hoping to get kids to buy their black down jackets from us instead of The North Face or Timberland. We want customers who *need* our clothing, not just desire it.

We don't want to be a big company. We want to be the best company, and it's easier to try to be the best small company than the best big company. We have to practice self-control. Growth in one part of the company may have to be sacrificed to allow growth in another. It's also important that we have a clear idea of what the limits are to this "experiment" and live within those limits, knowing that the sooner we expand outside them, the sooner the type of company we want will die.

Slow growth or no growth means the profits have to come from our being more efficient every year. Unlike the government, we cannot rely on an expanding economy to "burn the fat away." It's easier for a company to make a profit when it's growing at 10 percent or 20 percent a year. We have been profitable in years when we grew only a few percent by increasing the quality of our product, maximizing the efficiency of our operations, and living within our means.

Because of our pessimism about the future of a world economy based on limited resources and on endlessly consuming and discarding goods we often don't need, not only don't we want to be financially leveraged, but our goal is to have no debt.

A company with little debt or with cash in the kitty can take advantage of opportunities as they come up or invest in a start-up without having to go further in debt or find outside investors.

In an age when change happens so quickly, any strategic plan must be updated at least every year. Many Japanese companies don't do yearly budgets, they do a new budget every six months. In our case, an inflexible plan would be centralized planning at its worst. It builds in a certain rigidity, a certain bureaucracy, that is oblivious of changing realities. A budget can be a valuable guideline and planning tool, or it can be a bludgeon.

We have to look ahead in other ways as well. It's the role of financial people not only to tell you what happened but also to prevent rude surprises in the future. A company should always be playing "what if" scenarios—i.e., what if all our top management goes down in an airplane crash, our warehouse burns down, our main computer melts down or gets a virus? Or what if there is a 25 percent downturn in business or sales in Japan suddenly explode beyond our wildest planning? We don't need operational plans already set up to deal with these crises, but we do need to identify which one could strike so we are less likely to take a hit in the back of the head.

That same desire for transparency extends to our dealings with the government. We don't play games with the taxman or auditor. Our tax strategy is to pay our fair share but not a penny more. We don't, with clever advice, develop complex schemes to do an end run around our taxes. The same holds true for our accounting procedures. We know of legal ways to change how we account for our money, in inventory or expenses, for example, that would result in dramatically different reported earnings from one year to the next. In fact we could, within accepted and legal accounting practices, like so many public companies, show a profit every quarter. But our accounting strategy is to use only those techniques that, in the view of our CFO, provide the most accurate and consistent reflection of our true financial position.

We get approached by prospective buyers almost weekly, and their intent is always the same. They see an undervalued company that they can rapidly grow and take public. Being a publicly held corporation or even a partnership would put shackles on how we operate, restrict what we do with our profits, and put us on a growth/suicide track. Our intent is to remain a closely held private company, so we can continue to focus on our bottom line, doing good.

HUMAN RESOURCE PHILOSOPHY

A master in the art of living draws no sharp distinction between his work and his play; his labor and his leisure; his mind and his body; his education and his recreation. He hardly knows which is which. He simply pursues his vision of excellence through whatever he is doing, and leaves others to determine whether he is working or playing. To himself, he always appears to be doing both.

—FRANÇOIS AUGUSTE RENÉ CHATEAUBRIAND

Patagonia's working culture can be traced to the origins of Chouinard Equipment. Ours was a small company designing and making the world's best climbing equipment for its employees and their friends. The owners and employees were climbers; none considered themselves businesspeople. Working satisfied the creative urge to do something both useful and pleasurable, to make beautiful, functional climbing tools that the employees needed to pursue their own climbing. Work also satisfied the need to make money.

We had no dividing line between those who used the products and those who made them. The interest of the customer was equal to that of the employee. Climbers had a vested interest in making climbing gear. Patagonia's first clothes—rugby shirts, Stand Up Shorts—were made to climb in, and the employee attitude toward soft goods was no different from that toward the products made of iron.

Patagonia is of course a larger and much more complex company than Chouinard Equipment ever was. Most of the people who now sew Patagonia clothes will never wear them. It's our first principle of hiring, however, that as many Patagonia employees as possible also be true Patagonia customers. We like to use the clothes we design, have made, and sell, so we have a direct relationship to the product of our work. We don't try to "think like a customer," but *as* customers we get upset when a product doesn't meet our expectations, and we are proud when it does. I cannot imagine any company that wants to make the best product of its kind being staffed by people who do not care passionately about the product.

If Patagonia had begun primarily as a marketing idea or investment opportunity, the company would be a very different place to work. It would be understood that the primary purpose of the company would be the generation of wealth for its owners and investors. Working here might be much less an end in itself, more just a step in a career path.

Other values too can be traced to the origins of Chouinard Equipment. Most climbers of the 1960s and early 1970s, although middle-class and white, were alienated from the mainstream suburban culture. They valued their climbing time and their relationship to the rocks and the mountains, and they preferred taking physical risks to trying to get ahead in the larger world. Many earned subsistence incomes on purpose, and they worked as little as they could. Corporate life did not appeal; it was regarded as inauthentic, illegitimate, and toxic.

Patagonia employees have diverse political, social, and religious beliefs.

That's as it should be. And not everyone wants to change the world, but we want the company to feel like home for those who do. Employees who were drawn to Chouinard Equipment, and later to Patagonia, either shared those values or did not mind working among those who held them. Though their world has changed mightily since the 1960s, their residue remains here, chiefly in the commitment of so many employees to environmentalism, but also in our aversion to unnecessary hierarchy, unconscious material consumption, and a passive approach to life.

Kim Stroud, manager of our sample sewing shop, with a nonreleasable redtail hawk. Kim started a raptor rehabilitation facility at Patagonia that brings in injured or orphaned raptors. Volunteers assess them for injuries and illnesses, rehabilitate them, and release them back into nature. Nonreleasable birds are taken to schools in an education program. The Ojai Raptor Center takes in about 350 birds of prey each year. *Tim Davis*

Culture

The gatekeeper may be the most important person in the company.

—Doug Tompkins

If you care about having a company where employees treat work as play and regard themselves as ultimate customers for the products they produce, then you have to be careful whom you hire, treat them right, and train them to treat other people right. Otherwise you may come to work one day and find it isn't a place you want to be anymore.

Patagonia doesn't usually advertise in the *Wall Street Journal*, attend job fairs, or hire corporate headhunters to find new employees. We prefer instead to seek out people through an informal network of friends, colleagues, and business associates. We don't want someone who can just do a job; we want the *best* person for the job. Yet we don't look for "stars" seeking special treatment and perks. Our best efforts are collaborative, and the Patagonia culture rewards the ensemble player while it barely tolerates those who need the limelight.

We also seek, as I mentioned above, core Patagonia product users, people who love to spend as much time as possible in the mountains or the wild. We are, after all, an outdoor company. We would not staff our trade show booth with a bunch of out-of-shape guys wearing white shirts, ties, and suspenders any more than a doctor would let his receptionist smoke in the office. We can hardly continue to make the best outdoor clothing if we become primarily an "indoor" culture. So we seek out "dirtbags" who feel more at home in a base camp or on the river than they do in the office. All the better if they have excellent qualifications for whatever job we hire them for, but we'll often take a risk on an itinerant rock climber that we wouldn't on a run-of-the-mill MBA. Finding a dyed-in-the-wool businessperson to

The three-thousand-mile-long Great Wall of China was an early delusionary Star Wars defense.
It was built to keep out the Mongol lords, but they got in anyway by bribing a gate guard.
I breached it myself in 1980 by climbing over it. It's only 5.8 in difficulty. *Rick Ridgeway*

take up climbing or river running is a lot more difficult than teaching a person with a ready passion for the outdoors how to do a job.

Of course we do hire some people strictly for their technical expertise. We have employees who never sleep outside or who have never peed in the woods. What they all do share, as our organizational development consultant noted, is a passion for something outside themselves, whether for surfing or opera, climbing or gardening, skiing or community activism.

We've filled the choir with outdoor store clerks (lots of those), environmental activists, independent designers, white-water rodeo artists, journalists, car wash jockeys, fishing junkies, scriptwriters, painters, high school teachers, a municipal judge and several recovering lawyers, gospel singers, cabinetmakers, ski instructors, climbing guides, bagpipe players, airline pilots, forest rangers, computer nerds, a sprinkling of seasoned garmentos, and a few MBAs.

As the list shows, we value diversity of all kinds. Well over 50 percent of all jobs are held by women.

Hiring people with diverse backgrounds brings in a flexibility of thought and openness to new ways of doing things, as opposed to hiring clones from business schools who have been taught a codified way of doing business. A business that thrives on being different requires different types of people.

We hire slowly. We can afford to since we get an average of nine hundred applicants for each job opening. We make prospective candidates interview with their potential colleagues as well as their bosses. It is not uncommon for a management candidate to be interviewed by several groups of four to six people at a time or to return two or three times over several weeks.

As much as possible, we hire from within, to keep the company culture strong. And then we train, and take the time to train, as though our future depended on it.

These practices often demand extra effort in the short term: leaving a position unfilled while you scour for the right person, taking the extra time to train a river rat to do her new PR job, working with someone who may not share your language. In the long run the extra effort pays off—if you want to have an interesting, colorful, unpredictable place to spend your working hours.

This all sounds great, but the reality is that like most companies, we have to go outside the company to fill many top-level positions, including CEO. For some reason, we are still not doing a good enough job of training and mentoring our own people to grow into the ever more technical and sophisticated needs of a growing company. Maybe it's because we are still learning how to run a business ourselves!

Benefits

Remember, work has to be fun. We value employees who live rich and rounded lives. We run a flexible workplace, and we have ever since we were a blacksmith shop that shut down whenever the waves were six feet, hot, and glassy. Our policy has always allowed employees to work flexible hours, as long as the work gets done with no negative impacts on others. A serious surfer doesn't plan to go surfing next Tuesday at two o'clock. You go surfing when there are waves and the tide and wind are right. And you go ski powder when there's powder snow! And you better be "johnny at the rat hole" if you don't want to become a loser. This has led to our Let My People Go Surfing flextime policy. Employees take advantage of this policy to catch a good swell, or go bouldering for an afternoon, pursue an education, or get home in time to greet the kids when they climb down from the school bus. This flexibility allows us to keep valuable employees who love their freedom and sports too much to settle for the constraints of a more regimented work environment.

Our benefits package is generous but strategic. Each benefit makes good business

Some of our Ventura employees who take advantage of the "Let my people go surfing" flextime policy. *Chuck Journey*

sense for us. We offer comprehensive health insurance, even to part-time employees, in order to attract serious athletes to work in our retail stores. We provide on-site child care in Ventura, because we know parents are more productive if they're not worrying about the safety and well-being of their children.

When it opened in 1984, our Great Pacific Child Development Center was one of only 150 on-site corporate child care centers in the country. It includes an infant care room for children as young as eight weeks and rooms progressively for toddlers to kindergarteners. The Kids Club, for school-age children, picks up children at the end of the school day and brings them back to the GPCDC, saving their parents from having to make the drive and from worrying about after-school care.

The staff-to-child ratio in all parts of the child care center exceeds what is required by the state, and the caregivers are highly trained. The center has made a significant difference in the lives of the working parents in Ventura and their children.

It has an intimate bond with the company as well. Children's laughter and chatter are among the regular sounds of our business, from the playground outside, individual children visiting at their parents' desks, or full classes traipsing through the buildings on Halloween. A mother nursing her child during a meeting, commonplace in Ventura, is a regular reminder that the career versus child choices so many of us make in fact need not be choices. The child care operations continue to gain national attention, and the caregivers who run the center are often asked to help other businesses set up safe and nurturing on-site child care facilities.

What do the kids think? I walked into our child care building one day and asked some of the four- and five-year-olds, "Hi, kids! How's school?"

One young guy immediately corrected me. "We're not in school, we're at work. My mother works over there, and I work here."

What a difference that is from your average kid whose father or mother disappears every day for eight hours or more and who thus grows up with no concept of work. It's no wonder every young kid dreams of being "sponsored" by a big corporation like Oakley or Nike, as if this were what work is all about.

At Patagonia, our child care facility is producing one of our best products, excellent kids. The babies are constantly being held and handled by lots of caregivers; they are being raised by the whole village, with lots of stimulation and learning experiences. As a result, when a stranger says hello to them, they don't run and hide behind their mothers' skirts.

We encourage the kids to climb and fall and scrape themselves. When they're ready for kindergarten, their new teachers often comment that they are the most confident and polite kids in class. We used to let the kids go barefoot all the time—until we started getting complaints from their teachers that the kids refused to wear shoes to class!

There are about three hundred employees in Ventura and a hundred children in the child development center. We charge the parents rates that are lower than comparable child care centers, because we fund it with another six hundred thousand dollars in subsidies. What appears to be a financial burden is in fact a profit center. Seventy-one percent of our employees are women, and many occupy high-level management positions. Studies have shown that it costs a company an average of fifty thousand dollars to replace an employee—from recruiting costs, training, and loss of productivity. Our child care center helps us retain our skilled moms.

One cautionary note we learned: If you're going to have a child care center, you also need to give at least sixty days' paid maternity/paternity leave (we do). Otherwise many young parents still unclear on the concept of parenthood would rather dump the baby in the nursery as soon as possible and go back to work to pay for that new car or whatever. Those first few months are extremely important for children's bonding with the parents instead of child care workers.

Because we value healthy employees and social interaction among them, we run a cafeteria that serves healthy, organic, mostly vegetarian food. Most of the bathrooms have showers to accommodate lunchtime runners, volleyball players, or surfers.

Of course we offer generous discounts on employee purchases.

Peace Day celebration 2004. The Great Pacific Child Development Center is a participant in Jane Goodall's Roots and Shoots program.
Tim Davis

None of these benefits are particularly expensive for the company except, increasingly, health care. The child care program, with tax subsidies, pays for itself, and the cafeteria requires only a small company subsidy. Yet Patagonia is consistently included in lists of the hundred best companies to work for or for working mothers. Why on earth would anyone run a company that was *hard* to work for?

MANAGEMENT PHILOSOPHY

We've had psychologists who specialize in organizational development tell us that Patagonia has a far above average number of very independent-minded employees. In fact our employees are so independent, we're told, that they would be considered unemployable in a typical company.

We don't hire the kind of people you can order around, like the foot soldiers in an army who charge from their foxholes without question when their sergeant yells, "Let's go, boys!" We don't want drones who will simply follow directions. We want the kind of employee who will question the wisdom of something he regards as a bad decision. We do want people who, once they buy into a decision and believe in what they are doing, will work like demons to produce something of the highest possible quality—whether a shirt, a catalog, a store display, or a computer program. How you get these highly individualistic people to align and work for a common cause is the art of management at Patagonia.

Since we can't order our employees around, either they have to be convinced that what they are being asked to do is right, or they have to see for themselves it's right. Some independent people, until the point that they "get it" or it becomes "their idea," will outright refuse to do a job. Or worse, you get a passive-aggressive response so that you think the job will be done, but in the end the person just won't do it—a more polite but more costly form of refusal.

In a company as complex as ours no one person has the answer to our problems, but each has a part of the solution. The best democracy exists when decisions are made through consensus, when everyone comes to an agreement that the decision made is the correct one. Decisions based on compromise often leave the problem not completely solved, with both sides feeling cheated or unimportant or worse, as in the biblical example of Solomon, cutting the baby in half to settle the dispute between two harlots claiming the same baby. The key to building a consensus for action is good communication. A chief in an American Indian tribe was not elected because he was the richest or had a strong political machine; he was chosen chief because of his oratory skills, which were invaluable for building consensus within the tribe. In this information age it's tempting for managers to manage from their desks, staring at their computer screens and sending out instructions, instead of managing by walking about and talking to people. The best managers are never at their desks yet can be easily found and approached by everyone reporting to them.

Patagonia's offices support these ideas. No one has a private office in our company, and everyone works in open rooms with no doors or separations. What we lose in "quiet thinking space" is more than made up for with better communication and an egalitarian atmosphere. Animals and humans that live in groups or flocks constantly learn from one another. Our cafeteria, besides serving healthy organic food, is convenient for everyone and is open all day as an informal meeting place.

When you look to hire management, it is important to know the difference between leaders and managers. For instance, a branch manager of a bank is expected to avoid risk (not make loans without approval from higher up). Managers have short-term vision, implement strategic plans, and keep things running as they always have.

Leaders take risks, have long-term vision, create the strategic plans, and instigate change.

The best leadership is by example. Malinda's and my office space is like every-

An air photo of our one-square-block
facilities in Ventura, California.
Courtesy of Patagonia

one else's, and we always try to be available. We don't have special parking places
for ourselves or for any upper manage-
ment; the best spaces are reserved for fuel-efficient cars, no matter who owns
them. Malinda and I pay for our own lunches in our cafeteria; otherwise it would
send a message to the employees that it's okay to take from the company.

A familial company like ours runs on trust rather than on authoritarian rule.

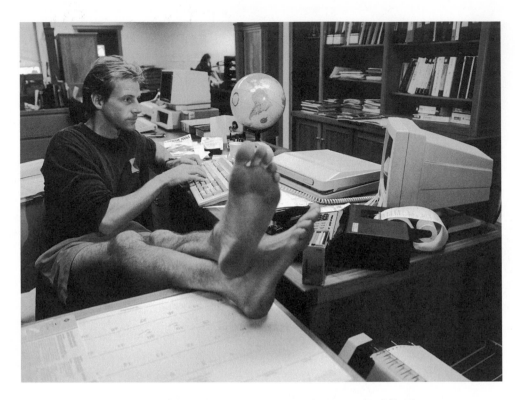

Who says that wearing a coat and a tie to work makes you a better worker? Kayaker, surfer, and now stuntman and rigger for Hollywood Bob McDougal at his desk. C. 1995.
Rick Ridgeway

Maybe a few people take advantage of our flextime and our Let My People Go Surfing policy, but none of our best employees would want to work in a company that didn't have that trust. They understand that my so-called MBA style of management (management by absence) is as much a sign of my trust in them as my desire to be out of the office.

Subscribing to the concept of natural growth of the company helps keep us small enough to be manageable. I believe that for the best communication and to avoid bureaucracy, you should ideally have no more than a hundred people working in one location. This is an extension of the fact that democracy seems to work best in small societies, where people have a sense of personal responsibility. In a small Sherpa or Inuit village there's no need to hire trash collectors or firemen; everyone takes care of community problems. And there's no need for police; evil has a hard time hiding from peer pressure. The most efficient size for a city is supposed to be about 250,000 to 350,000 people, large enough to have all the culture and amenities of a city and still be governable—like Santa Barbara, Auckland, and Florence.

Finding that balance between the management problems that come with growth and maintaining our philosophy of hiring independent-minded people and trusting them with responsibility is key to Patagonia's success. Every company also has its ideal size.

Although Malinda and I have always been closely involved in the direction and operation of Patagonia, we've always had a CEO as well. The fact that Patagonia has had six CEOs in its thirty years can be regarded as a failure to find and keep the right person (or as the failure of Patagonia's two hardheaded owners to relinquish power). Looking back, I see that each person brought with him a diverse set of skills that have been valuable to the company, whether he came from a background of retail, finance, biology, ex-Seal team, or education.

However, it's hard to find one person who can do everything well. For example, the "shoot from the hip turnaround artist" you hire to downsize your company may not be the CEO you need to run things after the company has been stabilized. And the person in charge of creating a new retail store usually has a different set of skills from the manager of a store that's been open and operating. The first needs to be expedient and creative, the second more nurturing.

A study done of the most successful CEOs in America (not the celebrity CEOs, but those who, without fanfare and jumping jobs every few years, get the work done) found one factor they all have in common: They enjoy working with their hands. The older ones had cars that they worked on in high school (when you could still work on your own car) or had wood shops in their garages where they made furniture. When a faucet needed a washer or a door wouldn't close properly, they did it themselves. When there's a problem of any kind, these people have the confidence to think it through and solve it themselves instead of looking for a "repairman." The longevity of a CEO's career is directly proportional to his problem-solving skills and ability to adapt and grow with the job.

When a problem comes up, the effective CEO does not immediately hire a consultant. Outsiders don't know your business the way you do, and anyway, I've found that most consultants come from a failed business. Only by confronting the problems and trying to solve them yourself will you prevent them from happening again in another form. The key to confronting and truly solving any problem is to continue to ask enough questions to get past all the symptoms and reach the actual cause, a form of the Socratic method or what Toyota management calls asking the five whys.

Here's a typical problem we experienced recently. Our sales in all channels of distribution in Japan took a 30 percent dive in November and December 2003. We asked why. Well, we had 20 percent of our inventory in puffy down and synthetic fill jackets because those had been the big fashion items the winter before and we expected the same response in 2003, but it wasn't happening. We started blaming ourselves for not being on top of the Japanese fashion trends, but we needed to ask more questions. Was business also down with other products in our winter line? Yes. We could have stopped here and come to the conclusion that Patagonia was out of fashion in the volatile Japanese market, and we would have started dumping our inventory of black down jackets.

But we asked more questions: How were the other companies and dealers doing? Their businesses were also down. Why? The weather in November and December was unseasonably warm. No one was selling winter clothing. So we hung on and didn't dump our inventory. In January it finally got cold, the ski areas got snow, and sales suddenly went up. We quickly sold out our inventory of cold-weather clothing without having to put it on sale. Had we acted after asking only a few questions we never would have gotten to the real cause: no cold weather.

The owners and managers of a business that wants to be around for the next hundred years had better love change. The most important mandate for a manager in a dynamic company is to instigate change. In his book *The Beak of the Finch* Jonathan Weiner talks about an insect that was found preserved in amber.

Lost Arrow Corporation and Patagonia CEO Michael Crooke and me talking it over at the "board room" off to the side of our surfboard-glassing shop. 2002
Courtesy of Patagonia

Ambassador Steve House climbing "light and fast" on Nuptse, Nepal. *Marko Prezelj*

The specimen, millions of years old, is identical in appearance to that species living today—with one big difference. The present-day insect has developed the ability to shed its legs and regenerate new ones after touching plants covered with pesticides. Surprisingly, this ability has evolved just since the time of World War II, when pesticide use began. The lesson to be learned is that evolution (change) doesn't happen without stress, and it can happen quickly.

The 48 percent of the American population who don't believe in the process of evolution, the evangelical conservatives who believe the earth and its creatures were created by God only ten thousand years ago, see change as a threat rather than an opportunity to grow and evolve to a higher level.

Climbing mountains is another process that serves as an example for both business and life. Many people don't understand that how you climb a mountain is more important than reaching the top. You can solo climb Everest without using oxygen, or you can pay guides and Sherpas to carry your loads, put ladders across crevasses, lay in six thousand feet of fixed ropes, and have one Sherpa pulling and one pushing you. You just dial in "10,000 Feet" on your oxygen bottle, and up you go.

Typical high-powered, rich plastic surgeons and CEOs who attempt to climb Everest this way are so fixated on the target, the summit, that they compromise on the process. The goal of climbing big, dangerous mountains should be to attain some sort of spiritual and personal growth, but this won't happen if you compromise away the entire process.

Just as doing risk sports will create stresses that lead to a bettering of one's self, so should a company constantly stress itself in order to grow. Our company has always done its best work whenever we've had a crisis. I've never been so proud of our employees as in 1994, when the entire company was mobilized to change over from using traditional cotton to organically grown by 1996. It was crisis that led to writing down our philosophies. When there is no crisis, the wise leader or CEO will invent one. Not by crying wolf but by challenging the employees with change.

As Bob Dylan says, "He not busy being born is busy dying."

New employees coming into a company with a strong culture and values may think that they shouldn't rock the boat and shouldn't challenge the status quo. On the contrary, while values should never change, every organization, business, government, or religion must be adaptive and resilient and constantly embrace new ideas and methods of operation.

ENVIRONMENTAL PHILOSOPHY

Anyone who believes exponential growth
can go on forever in a finite world is
either a madman or a politician.
—MIKLOS S. DORA, PARAPHRASING KENNETH BOULDING,
SURFERS JOURNAL

I'm a total pessimist about the fate of the natural world. In my lifetime I've seen nothing but a constant deterioration of all of the processes that are essential to maintaining healthy life on Planet Earth. Most of the scientists and deep thinkers in the environmental field that I know personally are also pessimistic, and they believe that we are experiencing an extremely accelerated extinction of species, including, possibly, much of the human race.

In Edward O. Wilson's book *The Future of Life*, he describes the time we live in as "nature's last stand." His "living planet index," which measures the condition of the world's forests and freshwater and marine ecosystems, puts humanity in crisis and at an environmental bottleneck of our own making. The twenty-first century must become the Century of the Environment, Wilson insists. If government, the private sector, and science don't begin to cooperate immediately to address issues of environmental degradation, the earth will lose its ability to regenerate. In other words, life as we know it is toast.

I'm pessimistic because I see no will in society to do enough about the impending doom. Yet there's no difference between a pessimist who says, "It's all over, don't bother trying to do anything, forget about voting, it won't make a differ-

Getting away from it all at the beach. *Jeff Devine*

WARNING

In 1992, a group called the Union of Concerned Scientists published a statement of its view of the state of the world. It was signed by over 1,700 scientists worldwide, including 104 Nobel laureates. Their warning says, in part:

> Human beings and the natural world are on a collision course. Human activities inflict harsh and often irreversible damage on the environment and on critical resources. If not checked, many of our current practices put at serious risk the future that we wish for human society and the plant and animal kingdoms, and may so alter the living world that it will be unable to sustain life in the manner that we know. Fundamental changes are urgent if we are to avoid the collision our present course will bring about.
>
> We the undersigned, senior members of the world's scientific community, hereby warn all humanity of what lies ahead. A great change in our stewardship of the earth and the life on it is required, if vast human misery is to be avoided and our global home on this planet is not to be irretrievably mutilated.
>
> Humankind is now in the first truly global crisis that concerns our survival as a species, the terms by which we might survive, and what it means to be human. No problem mentioned by the scientists is unsolvable in principle, if we have the wit and will to act with intelligence, foresight, and dispatch.

One all-too-common response to the warnings is to deny their validity. More sophisticated forms of denial are those that make the excuse we do not have the time or expertise to worry about issues beyond our special-ization. Beneath all forms of denial is the hope that someone else will fig-ure it out or that technology will save humankind in the nick of time.

> Global consumption of water is doubling every 20 years, more than twice the rate of human population growth. If current trends persist, by 2025 the demand for fresh water is expected to rise 56% above the amount that is currently available.
>
> —Maude Barlow, National Chairperson, Council of Canadians

ence," and an optimist who says, "Relax, everything is going to turn out fine." Either way the results are the same. Nothing gets done.

I also prefer to believe that in the most basic terms, evil is a stronger influence than good. By *evil* I mean something morally bad and destructive. Over and over I've seen so many institutions, governments, religions, corporations, and even sports become more evil when they could easily be doing more good. But believing this keeps me on my toes, keeps me from getting bit from behind, keeps me from becoming a victim.

Thinking these dark thoughts doesn't depress me; in fact I'm a happy person. I'm a Buddhist about it all. I've accepted the fact that there is a beginning and an end to everything. Maybe the human species has run its course and it's time for us to go away and leave room for other, one hopes, more intelligent and responsible, life forms.

I've found the cure for depression is action, and *action* is the basis for the environmental philosophy at Patagonia. Since our main reason for being in business is to work on changing the way governments and corporations ignore our environmental crisis, action is absolutely necessary.

I've always believed that the key to the government's doing the right thing is to base its planning on the premise that the society will be around for a hundred years. The Iroquois Nation extended its planning out even farther, seven generations into the future. If our government acted this way, it would not clear-cut the last old-growth forests or build dams that silt up in twenty years. It would not encourage its citizens to have more children just because doing so equates to more consumers. If I really believe in the rightness of such long-term planning, then Patagonia as a company must do the same.

When I think of stewardship or sustainability, I think back to when I was a GI in Korea, where I saw farmers pouring night soil on rice paddies that had been in continuous use for over three thousand years. Each generation of farmers assumed responsibility for leaving the land in better condition than when they took possession of it. Contrast this approach with that of modern agribusiness, in the Midwest, which wastes a bushel of topsoil to grow one bushel of corn and pumps out groundwater at a rate 25 percent faster than it's being replenished.

ONE SALMON

When the great river systems of western North America were created—the Fraser, the Skeena, the Columbia, the Sacramento, and the San Joaquin, to name only a few of the thousands—they were peopled with several kinds of salmon, fish of such grace, power, mystery, and pathos that some men have fallen in love with them as profoundly as with any woman.

In the extreme northeastern corner of Nevada there is a stream called Salmon Creek. As recently as a mere seventy years ago, maybe less, salmon came home here after a three-month journey from Astoria, up the Columbia and then the Snake River, to spawn and die in this peaceful, lovely high desert valley. When you walk along this stream today, there is an eerie feeling of loss, a palpable loneliness and sorrow in its very gravels, like a mother mourning for an eternity over her dead children.

This stream is not alone in its grief. The sorrow extends to countless other childless mothers in California, Oregon, Idaho, Washington, and Canada, mourning, moaning, wailing a hopeless cry of longing across the continent for their doomed children who can never, ever return because they are vanished forever from the face of the earth. Last year one solitary sockeye salmon reached Idaho.

In the not-too-distant past, when the salmon passed through the lower Columbia River, they were so numerous as to be utterly uncountable. Sometimes individual fish were actually shouldered out onto the bank, and this where the river was a mile wide.

Recently I stood on the terrible ramparts of the Bonneville Dam, a site where once a trillion salmon swam freely by, and I knew then where the devil himself lived, not in some imagined fiery cavern, but there inside the ice-cold concrete and steel. This was the epicenter of hell, where Satan could murder the river and its children again and again, ruling over an empire of satellite hells, committing similar murder. The roar of the strangled water was like a raging howl of fear and loathing.

I was asked to join a committee, and I did, knowing full well this was little more than waving a hankie in the face of a *Tyrannosaurus rex.* I considered explosives and legions of night soldiers, but this was clearly futile.

To neutralize the devil requires an equal force, the force of God. We are told He is not vengeful but, rather, forgiving. He said, "Vengeance is mine," but where is He when we need him to lean over this part of the earth and unleash from His out-stretched hand a torrent of fury and justice a hundred times the size of Krakatoa, the hydrogen bomb, and all the lightning bolts in history combined, setting off explosion after explosion, releasing vile gases and clouds enough to darken the earth for a century, as the devil's castles are blown to smithereens by deafening, blinding cata-clysms at Oroville, Shasta, Hetch Hetchy, Nimbus, Dry Creak, Pillsbury, Grand Coulee, The Dalles, John Day, Dworshak, Bonneville, and a thousand other places. The devil would return as always, but at least it might take awhile.

—*Russell Chatham*

Richard Grost

A responsible government would encourage farmers to be good stewards of the land and to practice sustainable agriculture. But why should only the farmer or the fisherman or forester have the responsibility to see that the earth remains habitable for future generations of humans and other wild things?

I can think of only a few examples of truly sustainable economic endeavors that can be done in any way other than on a micro scale. These are selective forestry and fishing and small-scale agriculture. Because these are essentially the products of sunlight, and the sun is free, it's possible to produce them without using up more material and energy than ends up in the final product (i.e., no waste). This sustainability also relies on the assumption that the main nutrient sources—soil and water—aren't being depleted by other endeavors.

The word *sustainable* is another of those words, like *gourmet* and *adventure*, that have been so overused and misused as to become meaningless. "Sustainable development" is far from sustainable, and "gourmet" hamburgers need not be very tasty to be so named. Every definition of *adventure* in Webster's denotes an element of risk, yet "adventure travel" is almost always risk-free.

A good example of a sustainable lifestyle was the salmon culture of the indigenous people of the Pacific Northwest, before colonization by Europeans in the eighteenth century. The salmon came into the rivers every year, and the people took what they needed, and no more. They let the rest go on to spawn and produce more salmon for the future. Their use of the forest was also sustainable because it was selective and was done on an appropriate scale.

Contrast this with the modern practices of salmon fishing, in which large diesel-powered boats run around the ocean catching both mature and immature salmon of mixed species, some of which, like cojo or steelhead, are endangered. The aggregate fisheries, even when they are targeting one species like the Fraser River sockeye in British Columbia, make no distinction among sockeye originating from any of the two dozen or so streams that make up the overall Fraser River runs. In some of these tributaries their runs have shrunk to only a few hundred remaining endangered individuals. One solution to the problem of a sustainable salmon fishery in Canada is to stop commercial fishing for salmon in the ocean, as Iceland has done, and let the fish come into the rivers, where they can be selectively caught with fish traps, fish wheels, and weirs. The nontargeted fish, like steelhead, can be released to provide a lucrative sport fishery. Another solution would be to use a fine-mesh tangle tooth net that holds the fish by their teeth and keeps them alive so the nontargeted fish can be sorted out.

Modern industrial forestry provides some of the best examples of nonsustainable agriculture. Modern forestry is considered agriculture, the reason why the U.S. Forest Service is under the Department of Agriculture and not the Department of the Interior. Our forests are treated as crops to be harvested, then replanted or allowed to regenerate on their own, to be cut again and replanted ad infinitum, a so-called renewable resource.

Clear-cutting is the most cost-effective method of harvest, and it gets rid of the undesirable undergrowth and low-value trees like the hemlock and alder. Then the land can be burned over and replanted in a monocrop like Douglas fir. The trouble is, nature doesn't like monocrops.

Clear-cutting, with its attendant road building (subsidized by the Forest Service), causes erosion, which silts up the rivers and destroys the salmon runs. The second-growth trees produce lower-quality wood and are more susceptible to diseases, such as the virus that is threatening Douglas fir farms in the Northwest. A third crop requires massive amounts of fertilizers, and it is doubtful that a fourth crop could even be grown, hardly the definition of a *renewable resource*.

Much of what I know about achieving any measure of sustainability in an economic activity, I learned in trying to grow my own garden. The land where I live happens to be part of the 90 percent of the earth where you can't do agriculture except for some limited grazing. My soil is a heavy, impenetrable clay. To break up the clay, I first had to double dig, breaking two shovel handles in the process. I had to bring in sand from the beach, mushroom compost (horse shit) from a local mushroom farm, and gypsum to break down the clay further. The soil is very alkali, so I had to add sulfur. It is also nitrogen-poor, so I brought in chicken, llama, and cow manure, plus composted sea kelp and worm castings from the worm composter at the Patagonia cafeteria and from our home kitchen scrap composter. I had to plant nitrogen-fixing clover and fava beans as cover crops. After years of effort I can finally say I have good soil that requires only the yearly addition of good compost. However, we would have starved if that had been our only source of food!

With all the addition of these amendments from the outside, my little two hundred square-foot garden may now be called organic but could hardly be called sustainable. In fact my soil is probably still lacking the five billion bacteria, twenty million fungi, and one million protists that reside in just a teaspoon of virgin topsoil. Nature has deemed that all these organisms are necessary for creating healthy new soil, fixing nitrogen, and releasing from bedrock the trace minerals that are so vital to human health. A study by the UK's Medical Research Council in 1991 showed that vegetables had lost up to 75 percent of their nutrients since 1940, meats had lost half their minerals, and fruits had lost about two-thirds.

The so-called green revolution of modern agribusiness, which relies on petroleum, is completely nonsustainable. David Pimentel, at Cornell University, has estimated that if all the world ate (and farmed) the way the United States does, we would exhaust all known global fossil fuel reserves in just over seven years. According to the *National Geographic*, it takes eight barrels of oil to produce one cow. Modern agriculture wastes topsoil at the rate of one inch a year, while it takes nature a thousand years to produce that inch of productive soil. In the Midwest a bushel of topsoil is destroyed for every bushel of corn grown. Agribusiness relies on massive amounts of fossil fuel fertilizers and toxic chemicals. It pumps groundwater for irrigation at a rate far greater than it is being replenished, and in the end it produces less food than can be grown with small-scale organic farming.

The Japanese farmer Masanobu Fukuoka, in his book *The One-Straw Revolution*, tells of producing the same amount of rice per acre as industrial agriculture without tilling the soil or flooding the fields or using any chemicals. John Jeavons at Ecology Action in California, using bio-intensive methods, reports that it has been able to produce four to six times more vegetables per acre than farms using mechanized and chemical agricultural techniques.

In my own garden I've never had to use any type of toxic chemical or artificial fertilizer because the plants are healthy and have a natural resistance to disease and insects. I rotate my crops, and I also mix up my plants to have diversity, so there is not the monocrop attraction to insects and disease. I also allow a hundred swallows to build nests under the eaves of my roof, so no flying insect has a chance of surviving my natural "air force."

When the Soviet Union broke up in 1989, the United States sent over a group of so-called experts from the ultraconservative Chicago School of Economics. Their idea for what to do with the failed, massive collective farms was not to turn them back into small, family-owned plots, but to keep them intact as giant agricorporations and sell stock in them!

Diversity and sustainability are vital to natural systems of living things, but it's not always clear how these traits translate into good business practice. We begin with the assumption that our business relies on natural resources to stay alive, and we are therefore a part of the system and obligated to maintain it. We embrace diversity and sustainability in all aspects of business.

At Patagonia the protection and preservation of the natural environment aren't just something we do after hours or when we finish our regular work; they're the reason we are in business. We'd have the same environmental philosophy if we were a cabinet shop, a winery, or a building contractor. I believe, as do most of our employees, that the health of our home planet is the bottom line, and it's a responsibility we all must share.

While Patagonia's other philosophies evolved out of our successes and failures in trying to be the "best" company, for the most part they apply directly to running the business. In a sense, they grew outward from our experiences inside the company. Our environmental philosophy evolved differently, coming to us from outside; it was the extent of the world's environmental crisis that compelled me to make changes at Patagonia. We're not only using less paper and electricity or making clothes from recycled materials but also going out into the world to work on solving those environmental issues that are putting the future of the natural world at risk.

A successful, long-lived, and productive company like Patagonia could be compared, on the most basic level, with a healthy environment, simply in the fact that both are composed of various elements that must function together in some kind of balance in order for the whole system to work. If we fill the earth's atmosphere with excess carbon dioxide and that causes a global rise in temperature, it also affects the oceans, forests, prairies, and everything and everyone living in those places. Correspondingly, if I were to change drastically one department at Patagonia without considering the effects on the rest of the company, the result would be chaos. No businessman in his right mind would, for example, intentionally cripple his accounting department without thought of the consequences to the rest of the company. Yet that's exactly what's being done to the environment; entire ecosystems are being destroyed or "converted" without consideration to the overall health of the planet.

Unfortunately, most of the environmental damage being done by business is the result of large corporations that aren't operating under the philosophy of sustainability, for either themselves or the environment. They're applying their own short-term business principles to a natural system that can operate only in the long term.

Neither government nor business uses full-cost accounting in its use of resources. In fact, the government's indicator for the health of the economy is the GNP (gross national product), which does not factor in the cost of goods; it only indicates sales. So, when there is a national catastrophe like a forest fire, war, or flood and resources are destroyed, the GNP goes up because money was spent on labor and materials. No debit is made in the national ledger for the loss of those natural resources.

It has been estimated that the true social and environmental cost of a hamburger when the forest has been cleared to create pastureland for grazing cattle is two hundred dollars.

Instead of adapting precautionary principles, we embrace new technologies, like nuclear power, genetically modified foods, pesticides, and other toxic chemicals with an attitude of "innocent until proved guilty," and it's left up to you and me to establish the guilt.

In the tropical rain forest, biologically the richest region on earth, we are exterminating species far faster than we can discover or name them, let alone determine their potential to benefit us in the form of medicine or food. More important, we don't know their role in the ecosystem and how their absence might disrupt it in catastrophic ways.

We do know that nature has already been disrupted, on a grand scale worldwide, in the form of global warming and climate change. However ingeniously adaptive and self-healing nature may be, human industry, especially during the past century, wreaks change far more quickly than nature can deal with it. Where we tip the balance, we yield desert, and at some point we may tip the balance planet-wide. At that point all mitigating human effort becomes, in Keynes's memorable phrase, "like pushing on a string."

We are the last generation that can experience true wilderness. Already the world has shrunk dramatically. To a Frenchman, the Pyrenees are "wild." To a kid living in a New York City ghetto, Central Park is "wilderness," the way Griffith Park in Burbank was to me when I was a kid. Even travelers in Patagonia forget that its giant, wild-looking estancias are really just overgrazed sheep farms. New Zealand

and Scotland were once forested and populated with long-forgotten animals. The place in the lower forty-eight states that is farthest away from a road or habitation is at the headwaters of the Snake River in Wyoming, and it's still only twenty-five miles. So if you define wilderness as a place that is more than a day's walk from civilization, there is no true wilderness left in North America, except in parts of Alaska and Canada.

We need to protect these areas of unaltered wildness and diversity to have a baseline, so we never forget what the real world is like—in perfect balance, the way nature intended the earth to be. This is the model we need to keep in mind on our way toward sustainability.

In a recent article in *Science*, ecological economist Robert Costanza argued, "We've been cooking the books for a long time by leaving out the worth of nature." The researchers compared the economic value of maintaining intact ecosystems versus exploiting them for economic gain. Specifically, they weighed the economic benefits of maintaining Thailand's wild mangroves and Cameroon's native tropical forest in their current states against the net benefits of converting them to shrimp farms and rubber plantations, respectively.

They found that the economic benefits of intact nature, in climate regulation, soil formation, nutrients cycling, and fuel, food, fibers, and pharmaceutical prod-

> In a true Earth-radical group, concern for wilderness preservation must be the keystone. The idea of wilderness, after all, is the most radical in human thought—more radical than Paine, than Marx, than Mao. Wilderness says: Human beings are not paramount, Earth is not for Homo sapiens alone, human life is but one life form on the planet and has no right to take exclusive possession. Yes, wilderness for its own sake, without any need to justify it for human benefit. Wilderness for wilderness. For bears and whales and titmice and rattlesnakes and stink bugs. And . . . wilderness for human beings. . . . Because it is home.
>
> —Dave Foreman, *Confessions of an Eco-Warrior*

ucts from wild species, outstripped exploitation by a conservative estimate of a hundred to one.

They also posited the question, "What would be the economic value of increasing the world's paltry annual outlay of $6.5 billion for habitat preservation to $45 billion, enough to create meaningful contiguous wild land reserves?" They estimated nature's resulting gift back to the economy at $440 trillion to $520 trillion.

Patagonia's environmental efforts began in the 1970s simply trying to prevent physical damage to the rock walls of Yosemite. It was about clean climbing and making high-quality products that weren't disposable. Later we started looking at minimizing the environmental harm associated with manufacturing our products. As we became more aware of the current crisis, we broadened our efforts to include correcting and cleaning up the potentially fatal environmental damage we as a society are inflicting on our planet and ourselves.

Our mission statement reflects this evolution by saying we will "cause no unnecessary harm," and it ends with our resolution to "use business to inspire and implement solutions to the environmental crisis."

This is an ambitious statement. To make it more than just talk, we had to lay out a framework, or a set of guidelines, to keep us on track. This led to the formulation of the most complex and far-reaching of Patagonia's philosophies, our environmental philosophy.

I would summarize the elements of this philosophy as follows:

1. Lead an examined life.
2. Clean up our own act.
3. Do our penance.
4. Support civil democracy.
5. Influence other companies.

12 June, 1994

To: Alison
From: Kris McDivitt
RE: Fun

Dear Alison,

Why wasn't FUN mentioned in the Mission Statement? I don't know, it's probably a good question.

Is it gone? Where'd it go? When'd it leave? Let's assume for a moment that you're right, having fun should be part of the culture at Patagonia. Certainly I would hope that people are, if not having fun, at least having a pleasant time working together. But if we're not having fun, let me look at this for you—let's blame it on Yvon.

He was the first one of us who knew that the world was coming to an ecologically disastrous end. He was the first one who knew we were all going down with the ship. He read the books first. He began to put the pieces together, certainly long before I ever knew you were supposed to do more than separate your trash for the trash man. Yes, I think it's Yvon's fault that we don't put "Having Fun" in our Mission Statement.

For you see, at least for me, it's difficult to keep our old rhetoric going and having fun, living like mavericks and gadflies, running like renegades of business and the like when the earth and most of her participants are in serious and probably irrevocable trouble. I know from personal experience that as soon as you begin to understand how close we are to SOME kind of natural disaster it changes your whole worldview. Even if you decide to simply do what you can and not kill yourself over it you still know what you know. Remember, within the company we proselytize this view every waking day, so it is difficult to carry the weight of that tough news around your neck in some form or another.

There's nothing keeping us from having fun at work and giving fun its due, we remember how to do it. But I'll bet you anything it's a new kind of fun, one mixed with a bit of a squint in one eye with our heads cocked toward the ground.

Lead an Examined Life

I don't really believe that humans are evil; it's just that we are not very intelligent animals. No animal is so stupid and greedy as to foul its own nest—except humans. We are certainly not smart enough to foretell the long-term results of our everyday actions. The brilliant scientist or entrepreneur businessman who invents or develops a new technology is often incapable of seeing the dark side of his ideas, whether it's atomic energy, television, or farmed salmon.

The problem is a failure of the imagination. In the sycophantic biography of George W. Bush *The Right Man: The Surprise Presidency of George W. Bush*, by David Frum, the worst thing said about him is that he was "uncurious." Uncurious people do not lead examined lives; they cannot see causes that lie deeper than the surface. They believe in blind faith, and the most frightening thing about blind faith is that it in turn leads to an inability, even an unwillingness, to accept facts. Consider results from a recent survey from the University of Maryland where researchers found that even after the CIA had issued its final report that there had been no weapons of mass destruction in Iraq, 72 percent of people surveyed who supported President Bush still believed that there were. An even higher percentage, contrary to all evidence, believed that Iraq and al Qaeda were linked.

Even more frightening than an electorate unable—unwilling—to allow facts to shape its reality is that it has elected a president and, to an increasing number of its members, a Congress whose views and policies are influenced by faith over fact. "For the first time in our history," Bill Moyers said in a recent speech at Harvard, "ideology and theology hold a monopoly of power in Washington."

Moyers went on to evoke the memory of James Watt, Reagan's secretary of the interior, who stated, in public testimony, that "after the last tree is felled, Christ will come back." Moyers then listed a few of the 45 senators and 186 members of

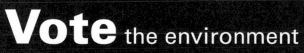

Your vote could finish the job.

The environment is in crisis.

This November 2nd, how we vote could determine whether American
children will, by the time they reach middle age, face life on a dying planet.
We can do better. But we don't have much time. Register. Get informed.
Vote the environment November 2nd.

Vote the environment

Check out: **www.patagonia.com/vote**

Congress who "earned 80 to 100 percent approval ratings from the three most influential Christian advocacy groups." These politicians are in office because they are supported by the growing legions of our population who literally interpret the Bible to conclude that the apocalypse is imminent. And people who believe the end of the world is around the corner can't be expected, as the journalist Glenn Scherer wrote in the online environmental magazine *Grist*, "to worry about the environment. Why care about the earth when the droughts, floods, famine and pestilence brought by ecological collapse are signs of the apocalypse foretold in the Bible?"

Students of anthropology won't be surprised by such developments. Frequently in cultures facing deep crises there emerge cults and movements usually led by messianic leaders promising to deliver true believers to a promised land free of the pain suffered in day-to-day life in societies facing collapse. Are Jerry Falwell and Pat Robertson the new messiahs? I don't think so, but if history is a guide, the emergence of one may be in our near future.

What should be our reaction? The only useful response is at every opportunity to preach as loudly and as forcefully as we can our own sermon of a reality in which facts trump faith. To recognize that most of the damage we cause to the planet is the result of our own ignorance; to recognize that we cannot afford to go about blindly doing unnecessary damage simply because we lack curiosity. Uncovering problems—and ultimately finding solutions—require not only allowing facts to influence your faith but also asking lots of questions, hard questions.

Most of the damage we cause to the planet is a result of our own ignorance. We go about blindly doing unnecessary damage because we are uncurious. Uncovering problems and ultimately finding solutions require asking a lot of questions. But I've found that asking one or two questions isn't sufficient; in fact that often leads to a false sense of security.

For example, if you want to feed your family healthy food, you have to start asking a lot of questions. If you merely ask, "Is this salmon fresh?" you may feel good about the answer. But if you follow that question with, "Is it wild or farmed?" or "Does this chicken have added hormones?" or "What do all those chemical ingredients mean that are listed on that label of Twinkies?" you'll start to reach the truth. Unfortunately the grocery clerk can't help you. You're going to have to educate yourself.

We had to do the same with Patagonia. We wanted to do the right thing, we didn't want to cause unnecessary harm, but in the beginning we hardly even knew what questions to ask.

One of the hardest things for a business to do is to investigate the environmental effects of its most successful product and, if it's bad, to change it or pull it off the shelves. Imagine that you're the owner of a company that makes land mines. You're employing people, and you're one of the best employers around, giving people jobs and benefits, but you've never thought about what land mines actually do. And then one day you go to Bosnia or Cambodia or Mozambique, and you see all these maimed innocent people, and you say, "Wow! This is what land mines do?" You can either get out of the land mine business (or tobacco or fast food) or continue, knowing what your products really do. So Patagonia started looking for its own "land mines."

In 1991, we began an environmental assessment program to examine our own products, and just as we had suspected, everything we make pollutes. But we all were surprised at how bad the news was; *sustainable manufacturing* is an oxymoron.

We conducted a life-cycle analysis of the four major fibers we use: wool, polyester, nylon, and cotton. Synthetics, such as polyester and nylon, are obvious villains because they're made from petroleum, but it turns out that the production of "natural" products like cotton and wool are no better (and in some cases worse) for the environment.

Let's take wool, for example. Wool can be very damaging or benign, depending on whether the sheep are grazing in fragile desert environments and alpine meadows or in areas with frequent rain, plenty of natural grass, and no predators. Wool also often relies on chemicals at every stage. The sheep are dipped in pesticides to kill parasites; the fleece is scoured with petroleum-based detergents; the yarn is bleached with chlorine and then dyed with heavy metal–based dyes. The workers exposed to the chemical sheep dips may suffer neurological damage. Orlon, a synthetic substitute for wool, is made from oil and is therefore not sustainable, so it seems that using any kind of wool would be a more natural and sustainable option than a synthetic substitute. But if you wanted to replace the output of one Orlon mill with wool, you would have to devote every acre from Maine to the Mississippi exclusively to the raising of sheep. In fact at our present rate of consumption, we can no longer clothe the world with natural fibers. Any attempt to achieve sustainability on this planet with over six billion of us is doomed to fail. But rather than shut the doors, bury our cars, and become hermits, we can work toward sustainability, recognizing that it's an ever-receding summit.

At Patagonia, we asked more questions. For example, were the neon-colored dyes used to dye our nylon toxic? After finding out what they were, we switched to dyes made in Germany that were less toxic in every color except orange, and we didn't do any more orange. For a company accustomed to simply ordering predyed fabric from a salesman's book, the question of dye toxicity added a level of complexity that changed the way we had to think. Most businesses wouldn't want to deal with creating "unnecessary" problems.

Most people, governments, and businesses don't want to ask the Toyota five whys because continuing to ask follow-up questions could lead to finding the real causes of their problems (more often than not environmental), which in turn would force them to make a change or be left with feelings of guilt. And there is money to be made in endlessly working on symptoms, like starting resource wars to protect our gas-guzzling way of life rather than work on energy efficiency or working to "cure" cancer with a pill rather than address its environmental causes.

I had a friend, Rell Sunn, who was an international surfing champion and one of the most elegant longboarders who ever lived. She developed breast cancer when she was just thirty-two. She traced her disease back to her childhood in Waianae, Hawaii, where there is an unusually high cluster of cancers. She remembered when she was a child, running after the "skeeter" truck that was coming back from spraying the sugarcane fields with DDT and other chemicals. The empty trucks would load up with water and spray the dirt roads to keep the dust down, while the kids hung on the back of the truck to cool off in the toxic spray. No one knew then what those chemicals would eventually do. Rell Sunn died of her cancer at age forty-seven.

Possibly the most graceful surfer there's ever been, Rell Sunn. 1993. *Tom Keck*

MAJOR COTTON PESTICIDES IN THE UNITED STATES

PESTICIDE CHEMICAL NAME (TRADE NAME)	AGRICULTURAL USE	IMMEDIATE TOXICITY
Aldicarb (Temik)	Insects and nematodes	High
Chlorpyrifos (Lorsban)	Insects	Moderate to high
Cyanazine (Bladex)	Weeds	Moderate to high
Dicofol (Kelthane)	Mites and has insecticidal properties	Moderate to high
Ethephon (Prep)	Plant growth/Regulator	Moderate
Fluometuron (Higalcoton)	Herbicide	Unknown
Metam sodium (Vapam)	Insects, nematodes, fungus, weeds	Moderate to high
Methyl Parathion (Parathion, Metaphos)	Insects	Very high
MSMA (Mesamate)	Herbicide	Moderate to high
Naled (Dibrom)	Insects; has miticidal properties	Very high
Profenofos (Curacron)	Insects and mites	High
Prometryn (Primatol Q)	Herbicide	Moderate to high
Propargite (Omite)	Miticide	Moderate to high
Sodium chlorate (Fall)	Leaf drop and weeds	Low
Tribufos (DEF, Folex)	Leaf drop	Moderate to high
Trifluralin (Treflan)	Herbicide	Low to moderate

Your typical industrial field worker.
Michael Ableman

Clean Up Our Own Act

We are the people we have been waiting for.
—NAVAJO MEDICINE MAN

At the time of our fiber study, we were manufacturing a lot of fleece jackets made from virgin polyester, the only kind of polyester available. So we worked with a company called Wellman to find alternatives. They developed a process that takes soda pop bottles, which are also made of polyester, and recycles them into raw material for jackets. It takes twenty-five bottles to make a jacket, and from 1993 through 2003 we diverted eighty-six million soda bottles from landfills. For every 150 virgin polyester jackets that we replaced with postconsumer recycled (PCR) polyester, we saved forty-two gallons of oil and prevented a half-ton of toxic air emissions.

Cotton is another story altogether, but it shows both the lengths we are willing to go to in order to do the right thing and the extent of the world's environmental crisis. Although cotton was grown without the use of chemicals for most of its known four-thousand-year history, today 25 percent of the annual worldwide insecticide use and 10 percent of the annual worldwide pesticide use are applied to conventionally grown cotton, even though cotton fields occupy less than 3 percent of the world's farmland. Many of these chemicals were originally formulated as nerve gases for warfare, so it's no surprise that higher rates of birth defects and cancer have been found in both humans and wildlife surrounding the cotton fields.

Knowing that there is a viable alternative, we chose to go organic. Not to do so would have been unconscionable; it would have violated our basic principle of making the best-quality product with the least unnecessary environmental harm.

But you don't just call the manufacturer and ask to be switched over to organic

Twenty-five of these polyester plastic soda pop bottles can make one PCR fleece jacket—if they don't end up along the side of the road or in a landfill. *Rick Ridgeway*

WATER ILLUSIONS

In the great Central Valley of California is a pond ringed with reeds and cattails. Although an artifice of rectangulation, the pond is peaceful, quiet, and a welcome respite from the miles of industrial cotton fields surrounding it. Standing water belongs in this place, a four-hundred-mile-long valley once rich with a vast mosaic of meandering wetlands, before dams and canals siphoned water from seven major rivers to quench the unquenchable thirst of the valley's farmlands.

There is a man standing by this pond. He is holding a gun. He is not a hunter or a bandit. He is an employee of the state who has been hired to fire his gun in the air any time waterfowl approach the pond. Why? Because this seemingly innocent body of shimmering blue water is so contaminated with salts, trace elements, and pesticides from agricultural runoff, it's more of a toxic soup than a pond. If birds spend any time here, they either die or produce offspring with multiple beaks and no eyes.

If irrigation, fertilization, and pest control practices contaminated only sitting ponds, the problem would at least be isolated. But they don't. In the Central Valley thousands of acres of rivers, streams, and estuaries carry elevated pesticide levels. So does the groundwater. Much of the population of this region relies upon groundwater as its only supply of drinking water. Contaminated drinking water means health risks to humans. Certain pesticides, some of which take decades to disappear from the ecosystem, significantly increase the risk of cancer and reduce fertility.

If the earth is the bones, then water is the marrow of this planet body. Marrow, according to the *Oxford English Dictionary,* is "the vital or essential part," which is to say, the goodness of a thing—the pith of a plant, the pulp of a fruit. Yet in all its goodness, water is tricky. It can take the shape of ice, fog, snow, and mud puddles. It can look as if it's there when it's not. But this time we've tricked water. We've made it look like a pond when it's not. Pesticides are poisoning our marrow, our goodness.

—Joanne Donman

cotton. Our decision began a long process of self-education. First, we found that very little certified organic cotton was being grown anywhere in the world. Organic farming is much more labor-intensive; the farmers must work the fields constantly, checking for hazards to plant health. Weeding and composting also require extra labor. Defoliation has to be done naturally, without toxic chemicals, so the mechanical cotton pickers can then be used.

After the organically grown cotton leaves the field, nearly every step in production—ginning, spinning, and knitting or weaving—incurs greater costs. Because of the limited demand, higher-per-pound cotton prices, the greater cost of using nontoxic defoliants, and the fact that raw cotton is not as clean to work with, the overall price of organic cotton is subsequently 50 to 100 percent higher. Nevertheless, in the summer of 1994 our board of directors voted that all conventionally grown cotton had to be eliminated by the spring of 1996.

At the time, sportswear made from cotton was 20 percent of our total business, and for the company to change to organic cotton had a huge emotional and financial price. The probable loss of revenue and profit because of the higher cost of organics was a great unknown.

We dropped some successful cotton products because we couldn't develop the fabrics, and we feverishly prepared ourselves for the switch. Many of our existing fabric vendors refused to participate in our process of switching over to organic cotton, mostly because of a lack of alternative suppliers and their skepticism about the market potential. The staff at Patagonia had to go back all the way to the beginning of the supply chain. We searched out cotton brokers with access to bales of organic cotton. Of all the fabric mills we ended up using for our supply of organic cotton, only two had had prior experience working with it. We had to pay three times more for our cotton fabric in 1996 than it cost in 1995, and there were fewer types available. We cut the cotton product line accordingly, from ninety-one styles down to sixty-six.

Two decisions facilitated our switch to organic products. First, we decided to use "transitional" cotton temporarily as well as certified organic. Transitional cotton is grown using all the organic processes, but the practices haven't been in place long enough to earn official certification. Second, we decided that we would sell "clothing made with organically grown cotton" rather than "organic clothing." The difference seems small, but we didn't want to mislead buyers about the fact that we would still be using synthetic dyes and conventional cotton thread in the production. We had found that natural dyes not only failed to meet our quality standards but had significant environmental problems of their own. Cotton thread is a mass-produced product that would require us to order huge minimum quantities of unknown quality. Further, while we learned and experimented with the new materials, we used a low formaldehyde resin in two styles for 1996 to minimize wrinkling and shrinkage.

Once again, we struggled with the conflict between our environmental standards and our quality standards. We faced the fact that it made no sense to turn around and put all the toxic chemicals back into the finished fabric to keep it from shrinking or wrinkling—two logical reasons why all those chemicals had been introduced to the material over the years. In fact a typical cotton product labeled 100 percent cotton is on average only 73 percent cotton; all the rest is resins, plasticizers, and chemicals added in the finishing process.

In the end, we solved the chemical problem by putting the quality back in the product construction instead of adding synthetic substances. In some cases, we had to use a higher-quality, longer-staple cotton and preshrink the yarn and fabric.

We realized as we switched over to organic cotton that we really didn't know much about how cotton as a material is processed or finished. In the past, when we wanted some fabric for pants, for example, we would call a salesman who would show us a sample book of fabrics, and we merely had to browse through and make a selection. Now we had to begin with bales of raw cotton and bird-dog the entire process through to the finished goods.

Meanwhile the marketing and sales team had settled on three goals for the spring 1996 organic cotton line: to sell the line successfully, to influence the rest of the apparel industry to use organic cotton, and to encourage growth in organic cotton farming. The last two obviously hinged on the first goal of having the product sell. We broke with our usual policy and hired an outside consultant, who confirmed our belief that the single most significant reason for a consumer making a purchase from us is quality. Brand name and price were secondary, and environmental concerns were least important to the purchaser. The consultant also found that small increases in retail prices were acceptable, so we reduced our margins on most of the items so the retail price would not exceed two to ten dollars over conventional cotton. Items that could not meet this goal were limited to our own retail and mail-order channels to keep the prices down.

Our organic cotton program has been a success, but not just because our customers are making the same choice we made—to pay more now for organics rather than pay the hidden environmental costs down the road—but because our designers and production people now have to begin their work with a bale of raw cotton and follow it all the way through the process of becoming a finished garment. They had to learn how to make clothing. The extra effort translated into products that are carefully thought out, and as a consequence they sell well. The fact that it's a natural product is not the reason most people buy it, but it's an important "added value."

Every time we've elected to do the right thing, even when it costs twice as much to do it that way, it's turned out to be more profitable. This strengthens my confidence that we're headed in the right direction. Our environmental assessment program educates us, and with education we have choices. When we act positively on solving problems instead of trying to find a way around them, we're farther along on the path toward sustainability. Plus we are constantly discovering more things we can do.

Switching from industrially grown and processed cotton to organically grown is a positive step forward but doesn't completely solve the problem. Even when cotton is grown without toxic chemicals, it still uses an inordinate amount of water and cannot be grown year after year without permanently depleting the soil. When a cotton garment is worn out, it is usually thrown away. We have to dig deeper and try to make products that close the loop, clothing that can be recycled infinitely into similar or equal products. We have to accept the responsibility for what happens to each product when it reaches the end of its life cycle, just as a computer manufacturer should be responsible for what happens to its old-model computers that are no longer usable and are too toxic to send to the landfill.

In accepting responsibility for our products, we must look at more than just the major fabrics. Here are three examples of where we've had to find a way to clean up the effects of individual components of a product.

In Portugal, where all our flannel shirts are made, the factories that dye the cloth are located along a river near Porto. Each dye house takes in water and then pours it back into the river after using it, so by the time the river reaches the last dye house downstream, it's all black and polluted. This last dye house had to install expensive German equipment to clean the water before it could use it, but it also decided to run the water through the cleaners again before putting it back into the river. This dye house, the one that discharges clean water, is the one that we chose to do our dying.

Polyvinyl chloride (PVC) is a toxic, carcinogenic plastic used everywhere in our society. It's in the coating on durable vinyl luggage, and it's a plasticizer for printing on T-shirts. We spent years trying to eliminate its use throughout the company and have found a way to take it out of all of our products, the sole exception being the foam on the Lotus Designs life jackets and some print on T-shirts, but we are still actively working on that.

Antimony, a toxic heavy metal, is used in the making of polyester resin. Yes, those soda pop bottles that we make Synchilla fleece from have antimony in the plastic, and cola, according to architect and designer William McDonough, is a good catalyst for releasing the antimony. We are working on switching to antimony-free polyester, but as you can imagine, getting the plastic chemical industry to change is not easy.

Our effort to minimize the impact of our internal operations began in the early 1980s, when one of the maintenance employees asked if I knew how much it cost Patagonia to be lining every wastebasket with a plastic bag. We were spending twelve hundred dollars a year for plastic bags that just went straight to the dump every day. I told him to get rid of them. But he came back the next day and said the janitorial service refused to clean the unlined baskets if people threw away wet garbage, like coffee grounds or food. So we gave each employee a personal trash can for recyclable paper and made everyone responsible for disposing of his or her wet garbage in separate containers scattered throughout the offices. Soon after, we started recycling all paper, with everyone responsible for his/her own recycling as well. The result is a company-wide recycling effort that also saves the company money.

Another employee recommended eliminating the Styrofoam and paper cups used in our cafeteria and at the water fountains. Employees started using their own cups, and guests are handed porcelain cups for their coffee. This saves another eight hundred dollars a year. These amounts may not seem like much, but the important point is that each time we tried to do the right thing for the environment, regardless of the cost to us, we ended up saving money. These cost savings were only the tip of the iceberg. Reusing cardboard boxes in the mailroom saves a thousand dollars a year, using our recycled, reused computer paper on the child care center's diaper-changing tables saves twelve hundred dollars a year, and the list goes on.

After conducting an energy audit of all our facilities, we changed over to energy-efficient lighting, repainted several wood ceilings white to reflect light, and put in skylights and innovative heating and cooling technologies. This amounted to a 25 percent savings in electricity. All our company-owned facilities in California are powered by Green-e wind power. In 2005 we installed solar photovoltaic panels to power part of our Ventura offices. This is a million-dollar investment, but between the tax rebates and lower electricity bills, we should break even in only a few years.

Seeing the causes of problems within the scope of the company is difficult enough. Once we get out into the world, the task becomes much greater. We know, for example, that the conventional timber industry devastates forests, speeds the loss of biodiversity, and causes erosion and flooding of critical watersheds. One-third of the world's forests have been cleared for logging and conversion to agriculture, and they are shrinking each year by an area equal to the size of Portugal. Tropical rain forests are being cleared at the rate of one hectare (2.47 acres) per second, and half the tropical forest is now lost. We can try to stop this clear-cutting, particularly of old-growth forest, through activism, lawsuits, or electing the right politicians, but it doesn't get to the root cause. As long as a demand exists for forest products, the forest will be cut, and if we continue to demand petroleum and whale meat, we will eventually drill for oil in our wildlife refuges and whales will continue to be harvested.

As a company we work on reducing our dependency on nonrenewable resources until which time we can switch over to a less harmful material. We try to use only recycled paper and wood products, and we use alternative building materials for all our retail outlets and office buildings. We use wood only when nothing else will work, and then it is used, remilled wood or virgin wood from sustainable sources.

In contrast, our government's solution to our dwindling forests is to subsidize the logging and paper pulp industries and promote tree farms as a "sustainable" practice. Frame houses made with two-by-fours and two-by-sixes would never be built if we had to pay the true cost of lumber. In Europe, no one builds with wood because it makes far inferior buildings, and the governments don't subsidize the industry.

We're examining various options for construction of a new three-story office building in Ventura. I'm excited about one method that uses a totally different process. This type of building construction is fireproof, earthquake-proof, mildew-proof, termite-proof, and energy-efficient and costs 25 percent less than a conventional building. It doesn't use any wood except for trim and window frames. It makes for a superior building in every way, and it's made from straw bales, a waste product. The fact that it's a more environmentally sustainable method is an added value. It's been estimated that with the amount of rice straw that is burned in the United States, you could build five million two-thousand-square-foot houses a year.

Any company environmental philosophy should also include the encouragement of employee participation at home. For example, while Patagonia has a tithing program to support environmental causes, we also have a matching funds program to encourage our employees to donate to their own favorite environmental and social groups. To encourage better fuel economy and to support the development of alternative vehicles, the company pays two thousand dollars toward any employee's purchase of a hybrid gas/electric car. We also allow employees to bring their home goods in for recycling. In 1989 our Salt Lake City staff took this commitment one step further by opening their parking lot as the first recycling station in the entire state of Utah.

Employees are empowered to get involved at all levels, either individually or as a group or department. They have the right to use company time to participate in Patagonia's environmental programs and to innovate new ones, as long as their regular jobs are properly done.

As an example, we recently had a big chunk of land in Nevada declared a wilderness, and this happened during the antienvironment Bush administration. It began when we moved our warehouse from Ventura to Reno, Nevada, and many

of our Ventura people decided to move too. When they got there, they realized that although Nevada had a lot of wild country and is 83 percent federal land, it didn't have much designated and protected wilderness. So they did an inventory of land and found 12 million acres that qualified. They started with the easiest, the Black Rock Desert area. Four employees came to us and said, "Look, if you continue paying our salaries and give us a desk, we think we'll have a wilderness bill within a couple of years." They joined up with the Nevada Wilderness Coalition, had both of Nevada's U.S. senators sponsor the bill, and went back to Washington and lobbied. As a result, 1.2 million acres of wilderness were protected for about ten cents an acre. In 2004 the coalition added another 768,000 acres of new wilderness.

John Williams and members of the Nevada Wilderness Coalition, assessing the North Pahroc Range of eastern Nevada, a proposed wilderness area.
Woods Wheatcroft

Snake River dam protest in Seattle. 2002. *Colin Meagher*

In the mid-1990s four people were arrested in a protest to save California's Headwaters Forest, a magnificent collection of ancient redwood groves threatened by harvesting. They were part of Patagonia's internship program, which allows employees to leave their jobs for up to two months to work for an environmental group and still receive their Patagonia paychecks and benefits. Under certain circumstances, the company will also post bail for those who have taken a class in civil nonviolent disobedience and are subsequently arrested in support of environmental causes. When a government is breaking or refusing to enforce its own laws, then I believe civil disobedience is the rightful course of action.

If you ask people today what they want for their children, they'll say they want to leave the world a better place, and they want to give their kids the things they didn't have when they were growing up. But people aren't making the choices necessary to make this rosy future happen.

Part of the reason no one will act is that people perceive themselves differently from the way others see them. SUV owners are a good example. They know that their SUVs are a bad environmental choice for a vehicle, but they rationalize it by saying they only use them for short trips or for carrying lots of people and gear. Or that it's a matter of safety, even though it has been proved that SUVs are *less* safe. Besides, they say, it's just one car. Other people, however, see SUV owners as a big part of the problem. The governments we choose, and the policies they set, are partly to blame for the environmentally harmful choices Americans make. If oil weren't so heavily subsidized and we had to pay the true cost of gasoline, then SUVs wouldn't be in demand and wouldn't be manufactured. Everyone would be driving a hybrid or alternative fuel vehicle or advocating high-speed trains. But when we go to the gas pump, we don't pay for the environmental damage or for the cost to protect our oil interests overseas.

Alternative or renewable fuel and energy sources can't compete with subsidized oil. Artificially cheap oil affects research and innovation in other industries as well. In a clothing business like Patagonia, where we use postconsumer recycled

(PCR) polyester, it's still cheaper to buy new polyester produced from oil. But it won't be for much longer, as the world runs out of oil.

When my generation was young, we were unaware that the health of our planet was endangered, and certainly no one imagined that one day a business would need an environmental as well as a financial policy. Not until Rachel Carson's book *Silent Spring* came out in 1962 did some of us awake from our torpor. Today most Americans are aware we are facing an environmental crisis. In surveys, 75 percent identify themselves as environmentalists. But you are what you do, not what you say you are.

We continue to blame others: the Mexicans for having large families, the Chinese for burning high-sulfur coal, or "the government" for wanting to drill for oil in the Arctic National Wildlife Refuge. Meanwhile we drive around in our SUVs, shopping and consuming like "good" Americans so the economy doesn't go south. The thought is, I'm not the problem; therefore, I'm not the solution.

For our government leaders, the environment occupies less than 5 percent of the political agenda. In fact it was a nonissue in the election campaigns of 2004. Voters say they want a healthy planet to live on, but it's not proved at election time, when it takes a backseat to all the other issues like security, health care, the price of gasoline. It's even harder to solve our problems when our government is leading us in the opposite direction with subsidized logging, tax credits for resource exploitation and for gas-guzzling vehicles, subsidies for conventionally grown cotton and other nonsustainable agriculture, and the promotion of consumerism as the basis for our economy.

Of course our government agencies are not the ones that are actually out there drilling for oil or leaving manufacturing by-products. Environmentally most corporations are doing the bare minimum they have to in order to get by. They hire environmental attorneys to make sure they are in compliance with existing laws, some of which they helped write in the first place. Worse, they continually want to rewrite those laws in order to do even less. Profits and jobs take precedence over

"I've never voted."

"You can't be a surfer and not see the impact of pollution and sewage in the water. The ocean's getting hammered. I want to see change. I am voting for people who put the environment first.

I'd never even registered to vote. But this year I have. This November 2nd, get out and vote for what matters to you."

– Chris Malloy

Vote the environment

Register today at: www.patagonia.com/vote

patagonia®

everything, and they use "consumer demand" as the reason for building environmentally bad products.

Without laws, and watchdogs to see that the laws are enforced, they'll stop building those products only when the consumers ask them to, not before. The timber worker felling old-growth trees and the machinist making assault rifles for citizen use can't escape their responsibility because "it's all about jobs" or "I just do what they tell me to." It's the old "the customer is king, and we are responsive to our customer's needs" excuse for not doing the right thing.

As for their products, they believe in letting the market decide if they should exist or not. A company should be responsible not only for causing the least amount of harm to society and the environment in making its product but also for the product itself.

For instance, automobile companies say they will stop making gas-guzzling SUVs when their customers demand them to change, but they don't educate their customers about the true environmental and social cost of owning SUVs.

The difficulty of convincing people to act is evident from a walk-through of Patagonia's own parking lots and offices. SUVs are studded all over the lot, and people are wearing jeans and shirts made from nonsustainable fibers grown with toxic chemicals. Even here, where everyone knows how bad all this stuff is, environmental values are a hard sell. One hopes that the kids coming out of our child care center will do better.

Do Our Penance

No matter how diligent we are at Patagonia in trying to cause less harm to the environment with our business, everything we make causes some waste and pollution. So the next step in our responsibility is to pay for our sins until such a time that we hope we can stop sinning.

Right after the OPEC-caused oil shortage of the early 1970s, Japan and industrialized countries in Europe put huge taxes on petroleum, forcing both nationwide conservation measures and the development of more efficient industries. The United States meanwhile did nothing of the sort, and we are paying the price. In the three decades since, the standard of living in the United States has doubled, but the standard of living in Europe has quadrupled. As for the quality of life, which measures clean air and water, education, health care, crime prevention, and other similar factors, the United States is now ten countries down the list from the top. Another result of the long-term energy policies of those countries is that they can now produce industrial goods using far less energy than U.S. companies require.

If the United States were to start taxing polluters, stop subsidizing such wasteful industries

BORN TO BE BAD

Limited liability corporations first came into use during the 18th and 19th centuries. They were designed to deal with the myriad of limits exceeded by our culture's social and economic system.

The railroads and other early corporations were simply too big and too technical to be built or insured by the incorporator's investments alone. When corporations failed, as they often did, the incorporators did not have the wealth to cover the damage. No one did. Thus, a limit was placed on the investor's liability, on the amount of damage for which they could be held liable.

Limited liability has allowed several generations of corporation owners to economically, psychologically, and legally ignore the limits of toxics, fisheries depletion, debt, and so on.

To expect corporations to function any differently is to engage in make-believe. We may as well expect a clock to cook, a car to give birth, or a gun to plant flowers. The specific and explicit function of for-profit corporations is to amass wealth. The function is not to guarantee that children are raised in environments free of toxic chemicals, nor to respect the autonomy or existence of indigenous peoples, not to protect the vocational or personal integrity of workers, nor to design safe modes of transportation, nor to support life on this planet. Nor is the function to serve communities. It never has been and never will be.

To expect corporations to do anything other than

amass wealth is to ignore our culture's entire history, current practices, current power structure and its system of rewards. It is to ignore everything we know about behavior modification: we reward those investing in or running corporations for what they do, and can therefore expect them to do it again. To expect those who hide behind corporate shields to do otherwise is delusional.

Limited liability corporations are institutions created explicitly to separate humans from the effects of their actions—making them, by definition, inhuman and inhumane. To the degree that we desire to live in a human and humane world—and, really, to the degree that we wish to survive—limited-liability corporations need to be eliminated.

—Derrick Jensen
(This article first appeared in the
March 2003 issue of the Ecologist,
www.theecologist.org)

as oil, timber, and industrial agriculture, put levy taxes on all nonrenewable resources, and correspondingly reduce the taxes on income, it would be the biggest step we could make toward becoming a sustainable society.

Closer to home, if I really believe in such thinking, then Patagonia, which consumes these resources and pollutes, cannot wait for the government to change. We have to tax ourselves and use those moneys to try to do some good.

In the early 1980s we started pledging 2 percent of our profits, before taxes, to nonprofit environmental groups, and we increased the amount as we became aware of more problems and the need for our support became greater. We reached a level of 10 percent of the company's profits, the maximum allowed as a tax deduction, in 1985. This became a sizable amount, as we were profitable and we always reinvested the profits in the company rather than take out bonuses and dividends. Since we're a private company, we were able to do the right thing without having to justify it to accountants and stockholders. When this 10 percent approach was formalized as policy, the company changed forever.

In the late 1980s some other companies developed their own grants programs, and several matched our commitment to give 10 percent of their profits. But in some cases, their profits were artificially low. After incentives and bonuses were paid to upper management, on paper the "profits" were much less, and many high-volume companies with 10 percent pledges actually gave very little to nonprofit groups. This practice violates the spirit of philanthropy. The idea is to give generously and not to find loopholes to avoid giving.

We felt we were doing our share, and since others seemed to want to follow our lead, we decided to up the ante. In 1996 we pledged to give 1 percent of our sales, meaning that whether we made money or not, whether we had a great year or a bad one, we had to give. It became not so much charity as a self-imposed "earth tax" for living on the planet, using up resources, and being part of the problem.

Support Civil Democracy

Democracy works best in small, homogeneous societies where everyone has to take responsibility for his or her actions. Peer pressure obviates the need for police, lawyers, judges, and prisons. You are responsible for your own and your parents' "social security." Decisions are made by consensus and not by compromise.

In the early days of our country and until the end of the nineteenth century, we had three powerful social forces: the federal government, local government, and civil democracy. Of the three, I would argue that civil democracy has been by far the most powerful. Activists were responsible for breaking away from Britain in the first place. Civil democracy, funded by private philanthropy, fueled the two great social movements of the nineteenth century, the abolition of slavery and the struggle for women's rights.

Creating Yosemite National Park was not Teddy Roosevelt's idea; it was the activist John Muir who talked Roosevelt into ditching his Secret Service men and camping under the redwoods.

African American women and children who refused to sit in the back of segregated buses and stood up to the federal marshals finally forced the government to enact civil rights legislation.

Antiwar activity stopped the war in Vietnam.

If you read a newspaper on any given day, you will see that most of the gains we are making as a society are still being done by activist citizens' organizations. These activists are taking politicians and CEOs to court for their malfeasance. They are forcing corporations to clean up sweatshops, sell only sustainably harvested wood, recycle their computers, and cut down on toxic wastes.

Citizen kayakers and fishermen work to bring down the obsolete dams and let the rivers flow. Falconers brought the peregrine falcon back from near extinction. Duck hunters have done the most to protect waterfowl in North America.

People may be afraid of the term *activist* because they associate it with ecosabotage and violent protests, but I'm talking about normal citizens who want the government to live up to its obligation to protect our air, water, and all other natural resources. Activists have infectious passion about the issues they support, whether they are mothers fighting to clean up toxic landfills that are killing their children or farmers losing their fourth-generation family businesses to urban sprawl. These are the people on the front lines, trying either to make the government obey its own laws or to recognize the need for a new law.

That's why our earth tax, 1 percent of our net sales, goes primarily to them. I've learned from a lifetime of being outdoors that nature loves diversity. It hates monoculture and centralization. A thousand activist groups, each working on a

Tom Cade with peregrine falcon. 1989. Tom went from being a founding member of our falconry club in 1954 to teaching ornithology at Cornell University, then starting the nonprofit Peregrine Fund, which has been responsible for bringing back the peregrine from near extinction in the United States. *Courtesy of Patagonia*

specific problem that it's passionate about, can accomplish much more than a bloated organization or government.

Whom do you trust to protect the remaining 5 percent of old-growth forest and the few remaining healthy salmon streams left in North America? The Forest Service? State and local governments? Corporations like Pacific Lumber or Weyerhaeuser? I don't trust any of them. The only ones I trust are small grassroots citizens organizations made up of people willing to tree-sit for months or stand in front of bulldozers. We need the river keepers, the bay keepers, the Forest Guardians, and the protesters who chain themselves to the front doors.

Worldwide, more than a hundred thousand nongovernmental organizations (NGOs) are working on ecological and social sustainability. In the United States alone over thirty thousand nonprofit organizations are addressing such

issues as biodiversity conservation, women's health, renewable energy, climate change, water conservation, trade laws, population growth, and wilderness protection. The fact that they all have arisen independently, without any common institutional framework, is a tremendous statement of the extent of the environmental crisis. Many of these grassroots organizations are far more capable of solving problems than are self-serving multinational corporations or government agencies. Most of them are local groups working long hours with minimal resources, and they are hanging on to existence by the thinnest thread, depending on small donations and fund-raising events like benefit auctions and bake sales.

This aracaria forest in Chile was due to be cut down for lumber. The local Mapuche indigenous peoples are dependent on piñon nuts for part of their sustenance. Doug Tompkins, Patagonia, and Allan Weeden formed the Lahuen Foundation to purchase and acquire the title to the land in 1989, placing it in permanent protection as the Cañi Sanctuary. *Courtesy of Patagonia*

Contemporary philanthropists and foundations shy away from funding organizations that promote advocacy or practice activism. With their meager twenty-five dollar donations these little groups have to stand up to the huge corporations and their teams of attorneys and to the government's biased judges and prostituted scientists.

Our 1 percent earth tax supports a wide variety of environmental activist groups and organizations. The major thrust of the Patagonia donations goes to individuals and organizations that are actively trying to save endangered rivers and forests, oceans and deserts. However, for every group we support we have to turn down three. To us, it's an indication of the depth of our problems that there are many more worthy causes than we can support.

One of the first purchases for Conservación Patagonica was the 155,000-acre Estancia Monte León. With its twenty-five miles of coastline on the Atlantic it is home to one of the largest Magellanic penguin rookeries on the Atlantic coast, along with sea lions, southern elephant seals, thousands of seabirds, pumas, guanacos, Darwin's rheas, and a variety of other plants and animals. On November 12, 2002, Monte León was officially made a national park of Argentina. *Courtesy of Patagonia*

Y.C., Kris McDivitt Tompkins, and Doug Tompkins in the Darwin Range of Tierra del Fuego, Chile. 2001. In 2000 we started a land trust (Conservación Patagonica) for the purpose of purchasing land in Argentina and Chile to create national parks and preserves.
Courtesy of Patagonia

The latest purchase of the land trust is the 173,000-acre Valle Chacabuco in the Patagonia region of southern Chile. The area is home to one of the few remaining concentrations of heumul deer. Valle Chacabuco connects two existing nature reserves, and its purchase creates a 645,000-acre area of protected terrain. www.conservacionpatagonica.org
Courtesy of Patagonia

These are the people who can make it happen! The 2003 Tools for Grassroots Activists conference attendees at Lake Tahoe. *Scott Willson*

Our financial contributions to activist causes have been significant (between 1985 and 2005 we gave twenty-two million dollars in cash and in-kind donations), but I've always thought we should provide them with more than just dollars. Among our other programs and in-kind assistance Patagonia holds a Tools for Grassroots Activists conference every eighteen months, where we teach activists the organizational, business, and marketing skills small groups need to survive in a competitive media environment. This is one of the most important services Patagonia provides. These people are often isolated, scared, and bravely passionate, and most of them are woefully unprepared to confront big business or big government with their teams of attorneys and "hired experts." By giving them the tools to present their position clearly and effectively, we do as much good as by giving them financial support.

Such efforts have incurred the wrath of conservatives, of course. In 1990 we were the target, along with twenty-four other companies, of a sophisticated boycott orchestrated by the Christian Action Council (CAC) because of our regular support of Planned Parenthood. Despite receiving thousands of letters from people saying they would never again buy our products, we coordinated a unified response from all the targeted companies—every one much larger than Patagonia. When we were threatened by the CAC with groups picketing our stores, we relied on a strategy called Pledge-a-Picket. We said that we would reward every picketer who showed up at one of our stores by donating ten dollars to Planned Parenthood in his or her name. They chose to stay away, and the boycott collapsed. We were described in the *New York Times* as "courageous," and we then received thousands of letters from Planned Parenthood supporters. In 1993 we busted a similar boycott attempt aimed at undermining our support of forest protection groups.

Hetch Hetchy. A dam that never should have been built and needs to be taken down. *David Cross*

We've had a few employees who didn't approve of the company's political beliefs and were greatly offended by our giving grants to family planning organizations. My answer is that they shouldn't be working for any company that they don't believe in, whether it's because of the product, like tobacco, or what the company does with its profits. And many new employees ask why Patagonia gives mostly to environmental causes, while, it would appear, we ignore social causes. The answer, I tell them (as well as the answers to nearly all the questions the company faces), can be found in the philosophies. In this case, the answer is found in the environmental philosophy itself. Focus on the causes, the philosophy tells us, not the symptoms.

Ex-logger, conservationist
Bruce Hill, with one for the pot.
Courtesy of Patagonia

WINNING ONE

In the spring of 1990, I set out with three other steelhead guides on a trip to the British Columbia coast in my twenty-two-foot sailboat *Reggae Nights.* Myron Kozak, Dave Evans, and I had looked at maps and were intrigued by a large river called the Kitlope that watered a large estuary at the end of a fifty-mile fjord. The Kitlope Valley seemed the remotest place on the BC coast. We were searching for steelhead streams, fresh crabs, and adventure. We found paradise.

We were stunned by the grandeur we found at the end of Gardner Canal: mountains rising seven thousand feet from the water, hanging glaciers, sheer granite walls, and waterfalls too numerous to count. When we arrived, there was a boat anchored in the estuary. Onshore was a crew laying out roads and landings. Despite my having worked in the forest industry for twenty-five years, subjecting this wild and wondrous valley to the industrial forestry that has compromised too many uniquely beautiful coastal valleys in North America seemed obscene. We decided then and there we would do all we could to keep the Kitlope in one piece.

We all had strong feelings about the environment, but only Myron had any real experience or connection to the environmental movement. We wrote letters to important people, but we were frustrated by our inability to communicate the beauty of the Kitlope to the outside world. That changed in the fall when I got a call from Myron telling me that someone called Yvon Chouinard from a Patagonia company was fishing on the Bulkley River. Myron, one of BC's leading outdoor photographers, felt that aerial photographs of the Kitlope would be the best vehicle to convey our message. Maybe we could talk this Chouinard fellow into hiring a helicopter and going into the Kitlope. I was given the task, and just minutes later I was in my pickup driving the 150 miles to Smithers to ask a total stranger for a considerable amount of money.

As Yvon walked up the bank from the river that evening, he recalled, "This big bearded guy in a logger's shirt approached me and said, 'Are you Yvon Chouinard? I hear you donate money to environmental causes.' I'm thinking, oh, God, a redneck logger and I can't even outrun him with my waders on."

I raved about the Kitlope, comparing it with Yosemite. After calming me down, Chouinard asked how he could help. I told him we needed pictures, good ones, and it was so remote a helicopter was the only way we could get them. He asked how much it would cost. I told him maybe as much as four thousand dollars. Calmly, Chouinard asked if the helicopter company took credit cards.

Two days later Myron was in a chopper with Yvon and his son racing for the Kitlope on a clear, crisp fall day. Myron was up to the task and took a vibrant series of aerial photographs of the Kitlope, pictures that eventually were published around the world.

Unknown to us, others were working for the Kitlope while all this was going on. The Haisla, whose traditional territories encompass the Kitlope, had a commitment to the Kitlope extending back thousands of years. What seemed trackless wilderness was their homeland and the birthplace of more than a few of them. They were desperate that the Kitlope be saved and were also struggling with how to do it.

A new environmental group, Ecotrust, was just in the process of forming with help from Conservation International. Ecotrust had identified the Kitlope as the largest unlogged coastal temperate rain forest watershed on earth. That summer Ecotrust (and Conservation International) founder Spencer Beebe had contacted the Haisla chief, Gerald Amos, and offered his help. Magic was afoot.

Myron's pictures of the Kitlope were sent to all the major international environmental organizations, and a set was given to the Haisla, who immediately set off to talk with the European owners of the logging rights (Eurocan) and show them what they were getting into. Myron's pictures began appearing in Ecotrust publications and magazines and newspapers. I was hired by Ecotrust to set up a community organization in Kitamaat Village, the Haisla community. The result was the Na'na'kila Institute. The combination of the absolute commitment of the Haisla to preserve the Kitlope and the sophistication of Ecotrust would prove formidable.

Ecotrust's forte is creating capacity in local communities. The impact the Na'na'kila Institute and other Patagonia-supported initiatives has had on Kitamaat Village is substantial. Nowhere are the links between social issues and environmental issues more immediate than on BC's coast. Canada's First Nations have been plagued by decades of paternalism and institutionalized racism and confined to pitifully small reserves. The effects have been shorter life spans, disease, poverty, and a shockingly high incidence of teenage suicide. Ecotrust's BC project director, Ken Margolis, decided to help and chose to assist a brand-new organization started by Haisla women, Haisla Rediscovery.

Rediscovery is an international program that assists local indigenous communities to set up children's camps in remote places. Started in Haida Gwaii twenty years ago, it uses traditional knowledge and elders to reacquaint children to their traditional cultures and land. The Haisla program was started by Dolores Pollard in response to a rash of children's suicides in Kitamaat Village. Using the Kitlope as a base for the children's camps, with substantial help for Ecotrust and the Na'na'kila Institute (and with funding assistance from Patagonia), the Kitlope was soon ringing with the songs of native and nonnative children. The bond between the Haisla and the Kitlope, always strong, became invincible.

At a conference sponsored by Ecotrust and chaired by the Haisla, Eurocan attempted one of the most astounding bribes in history. It offered the Haisla all the logging jobs in the Kitlope for fifty years. Not an insignificant offer since it was worth $125 million in wages to a community of 750 people with an unemployment rate around 50 percent. Eurocan was astounded when the Haisla didn't bite. In a profound display of commitment to the earth, the Haisla turned it down flat. Haisla elders confronted provincial bureaucrats, politicians, and timber barons and vowed that blood would run in the Kitlope if a single tree was touched. Within a year the new owners of the timber license for the Kitlope, West Fraser, relinquished all claims to the Kitlope without compensation. A complete slam dunk, a million acres of wild, unspoiled river was secured forever.

Patagonia gave substantial help to all the organizations involved in this remarkable environmental victory—Ecotrust, Ecotrust Canada, Na'na'kila Institute, and Haisla Rediscovery. In fact Ecotrust and Na'na'kila received the largest grants Patagonia ever gave, totaling about $150,000. While saving the Kitlope was the big win, there were even more victories. The Na'na'kila Institute was key in dramatically reducing the kill of grizzly bears on the central coast of BC, including a complete moratorium on their destruction in the Kitlope. Young Haisla men have been trained as conservation officers, and the Kitlope is now patrolled by Na'na'kila Watchmen. Dozens of Haisla have found employment in Kitlope-based programs.

The Kitlope is now a textbook case on how to create local capacity and conservation-based development. Without the help of Patagonia and other environmental grant givers, programs like these would be impossible. They do more than save wild places; they profoundly affect communities and people's lives. In this case, environmentalism was social activism at its best.

—*Bruce Hill*

The Kitlope. *Myron Kozak*

Our support of Planned Parenthood is an example. While that organization appears to be working strictly on social problems, Planned Parenthood actually works at the single greatest cause of our environmental problems, overpopulation. The countries with the greatest human misery are the ones with the highest birthrates. They are also the poorest countries. They are poor because the natural environment has been destroyed, as in Haiti or Rwanda. Even at a subsistence level, people clear trees for fuel and shelter and disturb habitat to grow food and build a house. Poor people, especially among formerly agricultural societies forced in increasingly large numbers to concentrate in cities, pollute and waste the natural world because they have no choice. Their soil and groundwater have been depleted; the rivers are dry or polluted, the aquifer drained.

Their birthrate will naturally go down when their quality of life goes up, just as it has in most developed countries. But a quality life won't happen until they can bring back the productivity of the land, until they start working with nature instead of against it.

Influence Other Companies

When Malinda and I made the decision to stay in business, we faced a personal challenge: Could we run a company that does much good and very little harm? Could we turn the company into a model, capable of effecting reform that we as individuals would be unable to accomplish? Could we actually change the way others treat the natural world? The environmental crisis is too big for one company, or ten companies, or one hundred companies.

If Patagonia can continue to be successful operating under the constraints of our environmental philosophy, then we perhaps can convince other companies that green business is good business and they can gain the confidence to take a few steps in the right direction. With luck this will lead other companies toward being part of the solution to the world's problems.

There are encouraging signs. Just as in the organic food industry, which is currently growing at a rate of over 20 percent a year, the worldwide demand for organic cotton is booming; it has tripled since we first made the switch in 1996. The farmers, gins, spinners, weavers, and cloth manufacturers that followed our lead all have created a new source of revenue for themselves. The costs of organic cotton have gone down to where it is on average only two times more expensive than industrial grown, and more and more companies, encouraged by us, are switching over. Several large companies like Nike, Levi's, and the Gap buy organically grown cotton to blend in with their industrial cotton as a way to support the organic movement but still not price themselves out of their established markets.

Some of the fiber mills we work with, at our prodding, are actively working on using less toxic materials and processes, like eliminating antimony and methyl bromide in polyester and trying to find a way of closing the loop with Nylon 6 polymers. They willingly work with us because they believe that what we are attempting to do is going to create a more sustainable business model for them and for society. They realize, as David Brower put it, "there's no business to be done on a dead planet."

1% FOR THE PLANET ALLIANCE

If you want to die the richest man, then just
stay sharp. Keep investing, Don't spend
anything. Don't eat any of the capital. Don't
have a good time. Don't get to know
yourself. Don't give anything away. Keep it
all. Die as rich as you can. But you know
what? I heard an expression that puts it
well: There's no pocket on that last shirt.

—SUSIE TOMPKINS BUELL

One fall afternoon in 1999 I was fly fishing on the Henrys Fork of the Snake River with Craig Mathews, the owner of Blue Ribbon Flies in West Yellowstone, Montana. We had been having a discussion about our realization that besides the fact that our respective companies were dependent on the existence of wild places in the world, we shared the personal belief that a healthy natural world is essential for humankind's survival. For both those reasons we supported grassroots environmental organizations through our businesses, even though we had anticipated alienating customers by taking stands on controversial issues. The turning point of our conversation came when we realized that both our businesses had actually grown because of our "radical" stands. It seemed unlikely that it was coincidental or that we had somehow drawn a few more radicals out of the woodwork to buy from us. There was something else at work: Customers wanted to support companies that not only took a stand on the environment but also took that stand by donating to activists.

The next part of our conversation was, How does a customer know which companies are donating to the environmental activists? We had both advertised our company's environmental stands, but it's not the kind of thing most businesses can put in their catalog, if they have one. It would cost more money to advertise their support than they could donate to causes. But what if there was a simple way to identify those companies— maybe a logo, like the Good Housekeeping Seal of Approval? Any business or individual could display it so that people would know where they stand on the environmental crisis.

Businesses donating 1% of their sales to the natural environment

In 2001 Craig Mathews and I started an organization called 1% for the Planet, an alliance of businesses pledging to donate at least 1% of sales toward active efforts to protect and restore our natural environment. 1% for the Planet is an organization devoted solely to increasing the effectiveness of grassroots environmental organizations by giving them more funding. The intent of 1% for the Planet is to help fund these diverse environmental organizations so that collectively they can be a more powerful force in solving the world's problems.

Here's how the alliance works: Each member company contributes 1 percent of its annual sales as tax-deductible donations to nonprofit environmental organizations. Members choose from a list of thousands of groups approved by and registered with 1% for the Planet. Each 1% member disperses its own contributions directly, which simplifies the decision-making process, minimizes bureaucracy, and encourages member companies to develop independent relationships with the groups they support.

In return, member companies then use the 1% for the Planet logo to communicate their environmental commitment to their customers. The logo allows customers to distinguish easily between green marketing and true commitment. Joining 1% for the Planet identifies a company as one that understands that the environment is the foundation for all life on

FOUNDATIONS

The urgency to tackle the environmental crisis through the funding of activists brings up the question of foundations and their role in all this. Foundations are required by law to give at least 5 percent of their assets each year. In 2001, in the United States, they gave nearly thirty billion dollars. That's a sizable sum, but considering the urgency of most problems and the fact that almost all have environmental causes, it may make more sense to give it away now when the environment is undergoing such rapid loss.

Most foundations were set up as testimonials to the wealth and character of those who established them, and as such they're usually under instructions to go on in perpetuity. But there's a strong case for giving more now, even giving away all the assets and closing up foundations. Like any investment that accrues over time, the realized benefits of immediate giving may be much more than giving a larger amount at a later time. This is certainly true for all of the rapidly expanding environmental problems.

Foundations, especially larger ones, become more conservative in time. If they have the money and the commitment, it comes down to the question of how to do the most good. If the purpose of a foundation is to convert its wealth into solutions for social problems, it makes sense to increase its giving to the point that problems are actually solved.

Besides, the founders may actually see the positive results of their giving while they are still alive.

—Y. C.

earth, including human civilizations, and that a healthy environment is necessary for all forms of life to have a future.

We chose 1 percent of sales because it's a "hard" number, not tied to variable profits, and it distinguishes us from companies who are using green marketing to promote their products. The vague declaration that a company is donating "a percentage of sales or profits" is meaningless; it could be one dollar or a million. 1% for the Planet means donating at least 1 percent. You can give more; Blue Ribbon Trout Flies is our cofounder and, though small, gives 2 percent.

Imagine if the president proposed that the next time you filed your income tax, the form had a place on the back where you could say, "I want 15 percent to go to this and 10 percent to go to that." People would jump at the opportunity to say where their tax money goes. Right now you have no say, especially if your party isn't in power. But if you tax yourself first, in the form of a donation to activists, you say where it goes.

Not many of us believe that our politicians or corporate moguls are going to lead us away from this apocalyptic environmental slide. It's going to take a revolution, and revolutions don't start from the top. 1% for the Planet is a self-imposed tax for using resources, but it's also an insurance policy that we'll still be in business in the future. I'd like to be able to get companies to give just 1 percent to the environment and to feel the same commitment and satisfaction that Mormons feel when they give 10 percent of their incomes to their church every year. Their tithing assures the church will take care of them if they should lose the farm.

For me, the solution to the world's problems is easy: We have to take action, and if we can't do it ourselves, we've got to dig into our pockets. The scariest moment is writing that first check, but you know what, the next day things go on: The phone still rings, there's food on the table, and the world is a little bit better.

As Mahatma Gandhi said, "You must be the change you wish to see in the world."

SUMMARY
SUMMARY

Dante once said that the hottest places in hell
are reserved for those who in times of great
moral crisis maintain their neutrality.

—John F. Kennedy

The Zen master would say if you want to change government, you have to aim at changing corporations, and if you want to change corporations, you first have to change the consumers. Whoa, wait a minute! The consumer? That's me. You mean I'm the one who has to change?

The original definition of consumer is: "One who destroys, or expends by use; devours, spends wastefully." It would take seven earths for the rest of the world to consume at the same rate we Americans do. Ninety percent of what we buy in a mall ends up in the dump within sixty to ninety days. It's no wonder we are no longer called citizens but consumers. A consumer is a good name for us, and our politicians and corporate leaders are reflections of whom we have become. With the average American reading at only an eighth-grade level and nearly 50 percent of Americans not believing in evolution, we have the government we deserve.

With our winner-take-all, nonproportional system of government in the United States and with all branches of the federal government and major media under conservative, antienvironment control, a lot of citizens are left disenfranchised. Now more than ever we need to encourage civil democracy by speaking out, joining up, volunteering, or supporting these groups financially so we can still have a voice in democracy.

When I look at my business today, I realize one of the biggest challenges I have is combating complacency. I always say we're running Patagonia as if it's going to be here a hundred years from now, but that doesn't mean we have a hundred years to get there! Our success and longevity lie in our ability to change quickly. Continuous change and innovation require maintaining a sense of urgency—a tall order, especially in Patagonia's seemingly laid-back corporate culture. In fact one of the biggest mandates I have for managers at the company is to instigate change. It's the only way we're going to survive in the long run.

It's the same in nature. Nature is constantly evolving, and ecosystems support species that adapt either through catastrophic events or through natural selection. A healthy environment operates with the same need for diversity and variety evident in a successful business, and that diversity evolves out of a commitment to constant change.

Our current landscape is filled with complacency, be it in the corporate world or on the environmental front. Only on the fringes of an ecosystem, those outer rings, do evolution and adaptation occur at a furious pace; the inner center of the system is where the entrenched, nonadapting species die off, doomed to failure by maintaining the status quo. Businesses go through the same cycles. Conventional corporations are at the center of the ring, and eventually they will die off, through either their own misdeeds or catastrophic events, such as dismal economic climates or unforeseen competition. Only those businesses operating with a sense of urgency, dancing on the fringe, constantly evolving, open to diversity and new ways of doing things, are going to be here one hundred years from now.

Claire Pennoyer Chouinard high up in a merlin's nest.
Cascapedia River, Quebec. 1987. *Courtesy of Patagonia*

Using the same metaphors for our own society, activists operate on those outer rings, nipping at the heels of conservative, complacent individuals living in the center. Those activists know if we don't act quickly, we won't have a planet to live on.

It's common thinking that nomadic people move when seasons change or resources run out, but they also pack up and move when the leaders see that everything is going too smoothly, when the people become lazy and complacent. The wise leaders know if they don't move while they are strong, they won't have the fortitude to move when the next crisis hits. Robinson Jeffers wrote, "In pleasant peace and security how suddenly the soul in a man begins to die."

Somewhere along the way individuals caused this whole mess, and it's up to us to fix it. If the world won't listen to me as an individual, perhaps they'll listen to the voice of a company of a thousand individuals. I can't reform the entire conventional farming industry, but I can ensure that Patagonia buys only organic cotton, and I can persuade other companies to buy it. We can work toward serving only organically grown produce in our cafeteria. If the demand for sustainably grown products were to become great enough, the markets would change, corporations would have to respond, and then governments would follow.

I don't have the courage to be a frontline activist myself. There are too many good causes that I support, and I get dangerously frustrated being on the front lines. But I believe in activism enough that I dip deep into my pockets and support those people with the courage to work in the trenches.

I have a different definition of evil from most people. Evil doesn't have to be an overt act; it can be merely the absence of good. If you have the ability, the resources, and the opportunity to do good and you do nothing, that can be evil.

The American dream is to own your own business, grow it as quickly as you can until you can cash out, and retire to the golf courses of Leisure World. The business itself is really the product, and it doesn't matter whether you're selling shampoo or land mines. Long-term capital investments in employee training, on-site child care, pollution controls, and pleasant working facilities all are negatives on the short-term ledger. When the company becomes the fatted calf, it's sold for a profit, and its resources and holdings are often ravaged and broken apart, leading to the disruption of family ties and the long-term health of local economies. The notion of business as disposable entities carries over to all other elements of society.

When you get away from the idea that a company is a product to be sold to the highest bidder in the shortest amount of time, all future decisions in the company are affected. The owners and the officers see that since the company will outlive them, they have responsibilities beyond the bottom line. Perhaps they will even see themselves as stewards, protectors of the corporate culture, the assets, and of course the employees.

Looking for somewhere to start? Go plant a tree. Only an optimist would do that. *Amy Kumler*

A certain void exists now with the decline of so many good institutions that used to guide our lives, such as social clubs, religions, athletic teams, neighborhoods, and nuclear families, all of which had a unifying effect. They gave us a sense of belonging to a group, working toward a common goal. People still need an ethical center, a sense of their role in society. A company can help fill that void if it shows its employees and its customers that it understands its own ethical responsibilities and then can help them respond to their own.

Patagonia will never be completely socially responsible. It will never make a totally sustainable nondamaging product. But it is committed to trying.

THANK YOU . . .

To my nephew Vincent Stanley, who ran wholesale, wrote catalog copy, and has been the historian of Patagonia, Inc. To Charlie Craighead, my editor and friend, who was miraculously able to organize my jumbled thoughts. To Doug Tompkins and Susie Tompkins Buell, who paved the way. To Kris McDivitt Tompkins, who for so many years did all the dirty work, and to all the great employees, past and present, of Patagonia who helped put into words what we believed to be true.

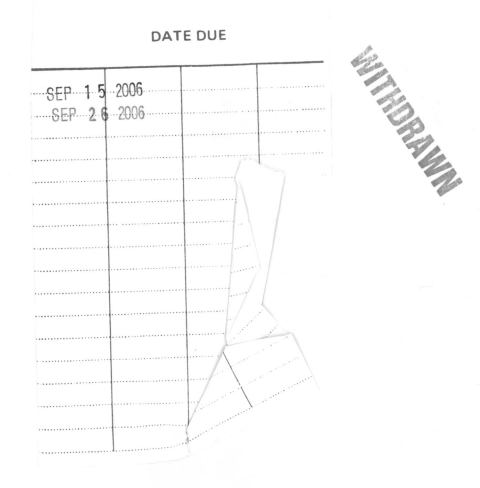